MISC

MIRIN
SESAME OIL
SM MALT VINEGAR
24OZ JAR POMODORO SAUCE
INSTANT POLENTA - YELLOW.

RED ENCHILADA SAUCE 16OZ

PANKO

15OZ COCONUT MILK X Q
PALM

1 CUP CASHEWS ROASTED.

TRISCUITS.
CORNFLAKES
15 OZ CREAMED CORN
15OZ CORN

EVOO

MISC

4x 32OZ CHIX BROTH
CIDER V
JASMINE
15OZ BLACK BEANS
28OZ CHOPPED TOMATO CAN (DICED)
CAPERS -
WHITE ANCHOVIES (CAN OR JAR.)
1 CUP PUFFED RICE
KETCHUP. - HEINZ
LENTILS DU PUY (FRENCH GREEN)
4OZ FLAT PACKED ANCHOVIES
1# RIGATONI
MAYO.
SOY SAUCE
28OZ WHOLE TOMATO CAN X 4
PIQUILLO PEPPERS JAR
GRAIN MUSTARD ⎱ MAILLE
DIJON MUSTARD ⎰
BREADCRUMBS PLAIN ⊗
1# SPAGHETTI
AP FLOUR LARGE
1 CUP DRIED APRICOTS - ORANGE ONES
SALTINE CRACKERS
AJI PANCA PASTE
QUINOA

FOOD & WINE CHEFS' EASY WEEKNIGHT DINNERS
EDITOR IN CHIEF **Dana Cowin**
EXECUTIVE EDITOR **Kate Heddings**
EDITOR **Susan Choung**
DESIGNER **Courtney Waddell Eckersley**
FEATURES EDITOR **Yaran Noti**
ASSOCIATE FOOD EDITOR **Ben Mims**
RECIPE TESTERS **Genevieve Ko, Sue Li**
SENIOR WINE EDITOR **Megan Krigbaum**
COPY EDITOR **Lisa Leventer**
SENIOR PRODUCTION MANAGER **Amelia Grohman**
PRODUCTION ASSOCIATE **Stephanie Thompson**
EDITORIAL ASSISTANT **Maral Tavitian**
RESEARCHER **Marissa Wolkenberg**

PHOTOGRAPHER **Fredrika Stjärne**
FOOD STYLIST **Simon Andrews**
PROP STYLIST **Suzie Myers**

FOOD & WINE MAGAZINE
SVP / EDITOR IN CHIEF **Dana Cowin**
EXECUTIVE MANAGING EDITOR **Mary Ellen Ward**
EXECUTIVE EDITOR **Pamela Kaufman**
DEPUTY EDITOR **Christine Quinlan**
DIRECTOR OF PHOTOGRAPHY **Fredrika Stjärne**
DESIGN DIRECTOR **Patricia Sanchez**
EXECUTIVE FOOD EDITOR **Tina Ujlaki**
EXECUTIVE WINE EDITOR **Ray Isle**

TIME INC. AFFLUENT MEDIA GROUP
VP, BOOKS & PRODUCTS / PUBLISHER **Marshall Corey**
DIRECTOR, BOOK PROGRAMS **Bruce Spanier**
DIRECTOR OF FULFILLMENT & PREMIUM VALUE **Philip Black**
VP, FINANCE **Keith Strohmeier**
DIRECTOR OF FINANCE **Thomas Noonan**
ASSOCIATE BUSINESS MANAGER **Desiree Flaherty**
SENIOR MANAGER, CONTRACTS & RIGHTS **Jeniqua Moore**

TIME HOME ENTERTAINMENT, INC.
SENIOR PRODUCTION MANAGER **Susan Chodakiewicz**

TIME INC.
CHIEF EXECUTIVE OFFICER **Joseph Ripp**
CHIEF CONTENT OFFICER **Norman Pearlstine**
EXECUTIVE VICE PRESIDENT **Evelyn Webster**
EXECUTIVE VICE PRESIDENT, CHIEF FINANCIAL OFFICER **Jeff Bairstow**
EXECUTIVE VICE PRESIDENTS **Lynne Biggar, Colin Bodell, Teri Everett, Mark Ford, Greg Giangrande, Lawrence A. Jacobs, Todd Larsen, Evelyn Webster**

chefs' *easy* weeknight dinners

100 fast & delicious recipes from star chefs

FOOD&**WINE**

Time Inc. Affluent Media Group

contents

18 chicken

21 herb-roasted spatchcock chicken

22 crisp pan-roasted chicken with anchovies, capers and lemon

25 butcher shop chicken

26 crunchy baked chicken thighs with grainy mustard and garlic

29 grilled chicken with miso-basil marinade

31 crispy chicken cutlets with swiss chard

32 flash-fried chicken carnitas

34 jw fried chicken

37 chipotle-braised chicken thighs with poached eggs

38 tangy chicken adobo

40 chicken hot pot

43 beer-braised chicken wings with clams and chickpeas

44 turmeric chicken and rice

46 peruvian-style arroz con pollo

49 healthy chicken jambalaya

50 thai chicken soup

53 roast chicken panzanella

54 pork

56 grilled pork chops with ginger sauce

58 chicken-fried pork chops

61 soy and ginger pork chops

62 pork blade steaks with sage butter sauce

64 pork and chorizo pozole

67 sautéed pork tenderloin with apricots and mustard

9 **FOREWORD**

12 **THE WEEKNIGHT CHEFS**

16 **WEEKNIGHT WINES**

68 ginger-braised pork meatballs in coconut broth

70 cheater's ramen with country ham, parmesan and egg

73 chorizo with rice and lentils

74 mapo tofu

77 italian sausage salad

78 beef

80 grilled strip steaks with green bean chimichurri

82 california steak salad

85 skirt steak with roasted tomatillo salsa

86 flank steak with chimichurri

89 rib eye steaks with grilled radicchio

90 "steak bomb" rice and beans

92 beef, turkey and mushroom meat loaf

94 lamb

96 salt-crusted rack of lamb

98 grilled lamb chops with cucumber relish

101 lamb shoulder steaks with ratatouille

102 spiced-lamb and potato pie

105 provençal lamb burgers

106 lentils with butternut squash and merguez sausage

108 fish

110 pan-fried flounder with lemon butter sauce

112 seared sole with lime sauce

115 trout amandine with creamy spinach

116 sea bass piccata with fried capers and leeks

118 crisp branzino with spinach

120 tuna steaks with plums

123 red snapper with asparagus and chorizo

125 halibut with roasted potatoes and romanesco salad

127 roast salmon with lemony basil sauce

128 quinoa-crusted salmon with spicy orange-miso sauce

contents

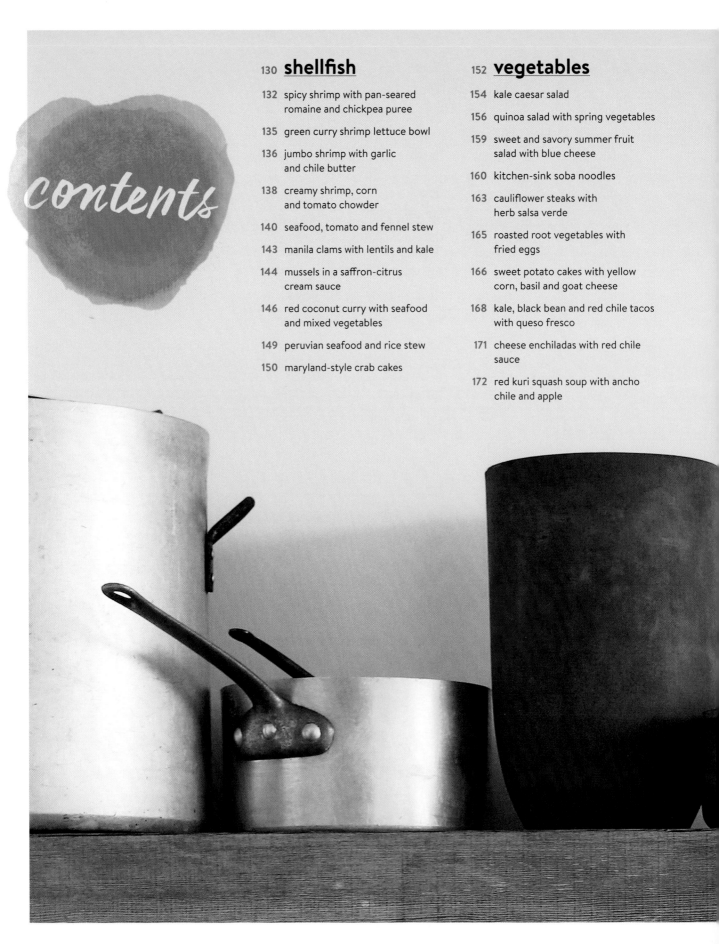

130 shellfish

132 spicy shrimp with pan-seared romaine and chickpea puree

135 green curry shrimp lettuce bowl

136 jumbo shrimp with garlic and chile butter

138 creamy shrimp, corn and tomato chowder

140 seafood, tomato and fennel stew

143 manila clams with lentils and kale

144 mussels in a saffron-citrus cream sauce

146 red coconut curry with seafood and mixed vegetables

149 peruvian seafood and rice stew

150 maryland-style crab cakes

152 vegetables

154 kale caesar salad

156 quinoa salad with spring vegetables

159 sweet and savory summer fruit salad with blue cheese

160 kitchen-sink soba noodles

163 cauliflower steaks with herb salsa verde

165 roasted root vegetables with fried eggs

166 sweet potato cakes with yellow corn, basil and goat cheese

168 kale, black bean and red chile tacos with queso fresco

171 cheese enchiladas with red chile sauce

172 red kuri squash soup with ancho chile and apple

175 chickpea-vegetable stew

177 winter vegetable minestrone

178 red lentil dal with rice, yogurt and tomatoes

180 **pasta and more**

182 spaghetti with veal meatballs

185 bucatini all'amatriciana with parmigiano

186 peruvian-style pasta bolognese

189 baked rigatoni with eggplant, tomatoes and ricotta

190 cauliflower and ricotta mac and cheese

192 creamy pasta with chicken and vegetables

195 rigatoni with lemony kale-and-pecorino pesto

196 rigatoni with clams, sausage and broccoli rabe

199 orecchiette with summer squash, mint and goat cheese

200 shrimp and wild mushroom risotto

203 sausage jambalaya

204 bacon and egg fried rice

207 farro and chickpea soup with chicken meatballs

209 pizza with baked meatballs

210 goat cheese and avocado toasts

213 baked polenta casserole

214 cuban frittata with bacon and potatoes

216 **desserts**

218 fruit and nut crumb bars

221 roasted peach cobbler with vanilla ice cream and balsamic syrup

223 rhubarb pudding cake

224 brown sugar crumb cake

226 mexican chocolate chip–pumpkin seed cake

229 oatmeal-cherry cookies

230 rosemary-cornmeal sugar cookies

232 dark chocolate pudding

235 popcorn pudding

237 **INDEX**

246 **STYLE GUIDE**

foreword

THE BEST CHEFS combine inspiring creativity with fierce efficiency, which is why F&W gave some of our favorites a challenge: Come up with delicious dishes for home cooks to prepare in 45 minutes or less. The chefs started with the recipes they turn to when they are pressed for time, or improvised and experimented until they came up with the quick and wonderful recipes here. Some are one-pot meals; others are easy to double and freeze. Many make smart use of secret weapons like chorizo and miso to add fast flavor to a dish, or call for canned ingredients, like creamed corn. By offering a glimpse into chefs' private lives—the healthy meals they make when they get home from the gym, the dinners they cook when extended family comes to visit—the recipes throughout this book show just how easily some of the best practices of restaurant cooking translate to the home kitchen. We hope you'll be inspired by all 100 dishes, and the ingenious ideas in each.

Dana Cowin

Editor in Chief
FOOD & WINE

Kate Heddings

Executive Editor
FOOD & WINE Cookbooks

> Play music and surround yourself with beautiful objects of permanence. Make your kitchen a magical, desirable place to be. —Edward Lee

the weeknight chefs

These are the chefs who shared their best weeknight recipes with us for this book. Here's a look at their styles—as pros and as home cooks.

cathal armstrong

Restaurant Eve, Alexandria, VA
restauranteve.com

pro cooking With its terrines and veloutés, Restaurant Eve is distinctly French, but there are nods to Armstrong's native Ireland in dishes like rib eye with Dublin spice and brown bread cream.

home cooking Armstrong's uncomplicated home recipes emphasize fresh produce, often procured from the 2,000-square-foot garden behind his restaurant.

  38 tangy chicken adobo

118 crisp branzino with spinach

175 chickpea-vegetable stew

192 creamy pasta with chicken and vegetables

rick bayless

Topolobampo, Chicago
rickbayless.com

pro cooking With a series on PBS and eight cookbooks, Bayless is America's foremost authority on authentic Mexican food. At Topolobampo, he might serve a Oaxacan black mole that takes a team of chefs hours to make.

home cooking "I don't have 12 hours to make dinner, so my food is small on fuss, big on flavor," Bayless says. While many chefs don't like cooking at home, "That's not me," he says. "I find it relaxing—and my wife, Deann, likes it."

  73 chorizo with rice and lentils

168 kale, black bean and red chile tacos with queso fresco

172 red kuri squash soup with ancho chile and apple

226 mexican chocolate chip–pumpkin seed cake

john besh

August, New Orleans
chefjohnbesh.com

pro cooking Besh is renowned for ultrarefined, incredibly rich dishes made with Gulf-area ingredients.

home cooking With four sons and a large extended family, Besh cooks for a crowd with just a handful of ingredients. "Easy cleanup is a priority," he says. "I don't want to make a huge mess, destroying every pot and pan."

  25 butcher shop chicken

190 cauliflower and ricotta mac and cheese

200 shrimp and wild mushroom risotto

203 sausage jambalaya

jamie bissonnette

Toro, Boston and New York City
toro-restaurant.com

pro cooking Bissonnette offers bold, thoughtfully composed flavors on small plates at his nose-to-tail *enoteca*, Coppa, and at his two Toro tapas restaurants.

home cooking At home, Bissonnette focuses on one-pot meals, "but not to avoid dishes," he insists. "I am OCD and really enjoy cleaning! I even fold my dirty laundry."

  43 beer-braised chicken wings with clams and chickpeas

  77 italian sausage salad

  90 "steak bomb" rice and beans

199 orecchiette with summer squash, mint and goat cheese

tim byres

Smoke, Dallas
timbyres.com

pro cooking A classically trained chef turned pit master, Byres is a rare barbecue guru whose expertise extends beyond smoky meat to vegetables and even desserts.

home cooking Byres loves to add smokiness to dishes with ingredients like chorizo as well as fresh flavors from vegetables (lemony asparagus, watercress). "I like punch and pop in my food," he says.

29   grilled miso-basil chicken

123   red snapper with asparagus

214   cuban frittata with bacon and potatoes

230   rosemary-cornmeal sugar cookies

chris cosentino

Porcellino, San Francisco
offalgood.com

pro cooking A pioneer of whole-animal cooking, Cosentino is famous for offal. An Italian peasant dish may feature lamb's head, for instance.

home cooking Cosentino sticks to more manageable cuts of meat, as well as chicken, pasta and fish, adding flavor complexity with assertive ingredients like anchovies.

22   crisp pan-roasted chicken

62   pork steaks with sage butter sauce

125   halibut with roasted potatoes

195   rigatoni with lemony kale pesto

rocco dispirito

Cookbook author
roccodispirito.com

pro cooking The wunderkind chef at the now-shuttered Union Pacific in New York City, DiSpirito currently uses his culinary genius to devise delicious healthy recipes for cookbooks like *Now Eat This!*

home cooking DiSpirito lightens up classic dishes with lean proteins and boosts flavor with bold seasonings like curry paste and adobo powder.

32   flash-fried chicken carnitas

49   healthy chicken jambalaya

92   beef, turkey and mushroom meat loaf

146   red coconut curry with seafood

renee erickson

Boat Street Café, Seattle
boatstreetcafe.com

pro cooking Erickson makes French bistro–style dishes with Pacific Northwest ingredients, such as razor clam beignets with parsley-and-caper remoulade.

home cooking Her style is rustic and relaxed: She serves white wine–steamed clams straight from the pot. "People have this idea that I cook at home like I do at the restaurant," Erickson says. "I don't. I'm more into hanging out."

89   rib eye steaks with grilled radicchio

98   lamb chops with cucumber relish

127   salmon with lemony basil sauce

143   manila clams with lentils and kale

susan feniger

Border Grill, Los Angeles
marysueandsusan.com

pro cooking Feniger helped redefine Mexican food when she opened Border Grill with Mary Sue Milliken in the '80s. At Mud Hen Tavern, she explores global flavors with dishes from Singapore and the Middle East.

home cooking Feniger's dishes are vegetable-focused and ultrasatisfying. "I love to cook way too much on a Sunday night so I can make something delicious with leftovers when I come home late during the week," she says.

160   kitchen-sink soba noodles

165   roasted root vegetables with eggs

178   red lentil dal with rice, yogurt and tomatoes

210   goat cheese and avocado toasts

tyler florence

Wayfare Tavern, San Francisco
tylerflorence.com

pro cooking Florence serves luxe versions of American favorites, like a burger combining ground prime rib, brisket, skirt steak and tenderloin stacked with bacon and triple-cream cheese.

home cooking "With family and friends and wine and music, my home cooking is relaxed," Florence says. "When people are paying for dinner, that's different."

21   herb-roasted spatchcock chicken

82   california steak salad

154   kale caesar salad

196   rigatoni with clams, sausage and broccoli rabe

colby and megan garrelts

Bluestem, Kansas City, MO
bluestemkc.com

pro cooking Colby Garrelts creates Midwestern-haute dishes like a *torchon* of foie gras with bourbon cream, candied cranberries and pecans. His wife Megan's desserts are just as ambitious.

home cooking "Restaurant cooking is like building a bunch of parts at a factory, then putting them together at the last minute," Colby says about the cuisine he and Megan serve at Bluestem. At home, he cooks boldly flavored meals, while Megan bakes Americana desserts inspired by her childhood.

86   flank steak with chimichurri

140   seafood, tomato and fennel stew

224   brown sugar crumb cake

229   oatmeal-cherry cookies

the weeknight chefs

(continued)

spike gjerde

Woodberry Kitchen, Baltimore
woodberrykitchen.com

pro cooking Gjerde is committed to Chesapeake Bay cookery: He prepares seafood from local waters and sells every cut of locally raised meat at his whole-animal butcher shop.
home cooking "I think about cooking smarter," Gjerde says. "I'll roast a chicken for dinner, pull off the remaining meat and simmer the carcass for stock to make my Thai chicken soup a night or two later."

50 thai chicken soup
150 maryland-style crab cakes
204 bacon and egg fried rice
232 dark chocolate pudding

alex guarnaschelli

Butter, New York City
butterrestaurant.com

pro cooking Guarnaschelli cooks lavish dishes that are all about abundance, like a mammoth 40-ounce tomahawk steak on the bone.
home cooking Her favorite dishes have a "high tang factor": She tops seared cauliflower with a piquant salsa verde and spikes root vegetable minestrone with red wine vinegar.

26 baked chicken with grainy mustard
101 lamb steaks with ratatouille
163 cauliflower steaks with salsa verde
177 winter vegetable minestrone

carla hall

Cookbook author
carlahall.com

pro cooking The former model and co-host of *The Chew* often lightens the Southern comfort foods she grew up eating and the dishes she's discovered in her travels around the world.
home cooking "I try to re-create the dishes from the Sunday suppers at my grandmother's house," Hall says. She adds her own quick twists, such as using creamed corn to thicken chowder.

102 spiced-lamb and potato pie
138 creamy shrimp, corn and tomato chowder
156 quinoa salad with spring vegetables
223 rhubarb pudding cake

matt and kate jennings

Townsman, Boston, opening in late 2014

pro cooking The husband-and-wife chef team are DIY masters. They spend days, if not weeks, making their own charcuterie, bread, pickles and cheese.
home cooking When getting dinner on the table, the Jenningses take shortcuts like grinding Triscuits and cornflakes to coat chicken cutlets or topping pizza with leftover meatballs and sauce.

31 crispy chicken cutlets with swiss chard
120 tuna steaks with plums
209 pizza with baked meatballs
218 fruit and nut crumb bars

mourad lahlou

Aziza, San Francisco
aziza-sf.com

pro cooking Lahlou is known for sleekly reimagined Cal-Moroccan cuisine informed by his childhood in Marrakesh.
home cooking The chef adds Moroccan touches in simple ways, topping stewed lentils with merguez sausage, say, and flavoring mussels in cream sauce with saffron and citrus zest.

96 salt-crusted rack of lamb
106 lentils with butternut squash and merguez sausage
132 spicy shrimp with pan-seared romaine and chickpea puree
144 mussels in a saffron-citrus cream sauce

edward lee

610 Magnolia, Louisville, Kentucky
chefedwardlee.com

pro cooking A multiculti innovator, Lee marries Asian flavors with Southern ingredients in unexpected and delicious ways.
home cooking Lee loves adding umami to dishes—for instance, by infusing a quick ramen broth with country ham.

44 turmeric chicken and rice
70 cheater's ramen with country ham
135 green curry shrimp lettuce bowl
159 sweet and savory summer fruit salad with blue cheese

jenn louis

Lincoln, Portland, OR
lincolnpdx.com

pro cooking Louis's seemingly simple dishes—she's famous for her gnocchi—are more experimental and technical than they appear.
home cooking "I like to eat healthfully and cook things I don't get to make at the restaurant," Louis says. She brings home the flavors of Mexico in a smoky chicken braise, and those of Thailand with meatballs in coconut milk.

37 chipotle-braised chicken thighs with poached eggs
68 ginger-braised pork meatballs in coconut broth

185 bucatini all'amatriciana
207 farro and chickpea soup with chicken meatballs

evan and sarah rich

Rich Table, San Francisco
richtablesf.com

pro cooking The husband-and-wife chef duo match incongruous ingredients in playful ways, pairing puffy porcini doughnuts with a raclette cheese dip.

home cooking "I cook every night for the family," Sarah says. "But if it were just me, I'd be eating cereal or grilled cheese." Instead, she and Evan revamp dishes in simple ways—for example, stirring sliced green beans into an herb sauce for steak to add extra crunch.

53 roast chicken panzanella
80 grilled strip steak with green bean chimichurri
115 trout amandine with creamy spinach
166 sweet potato cakes with yellow corn, basil and goat cheese

aarón sánchez

Mestizo, Leawood, KS
chefaaronsanchez.com

pro cooking Sánchez modernizes traditional Mexican recipes and invents brand-new ones, as in pepita-crusted scallops with a creamy corn sauce.

home cooking "I cook old-school dishes for my *tío* [uncle] at home," Sánchez says. His quick, accessible Mexican recipes include cheesy four-ingredient enchiladas.

64 pork and chorizo pozole
85 skirt steak with roasted tomatillo salsa
136 jumbo shrimp with garlic and chile butter
171 cheese enchiladas with red chile sauce

jonathon sawyer

The Greenhouse Tavern, Cleveland
jonathonsawyer.com

pro cooking Sawyer goes deep on the food he loves: A vinegar fiend, he's made it from everything, including mead; a french fry lover, he always has at least three versions on his international pub food menu.

home cooking Experimental but uncomplicated, Sawyer embraces superfunky cheeses and novel desserts.

58 chicken-fried pork chops
105 provençal lamb burgers
213 baked polenta casserole
235 popcorn pudding

jonathan waxman

Barbuto, New York City
barbutonyc.com

pro cooking A trailblazer and mentor to star chefs like Bobby Flay, Waxman is a pioneer of California cuisine.

home cooking "The dishes I make at home bear little resemblance to what I make at the restaurant," Waxman says. "With no need to be fancy, it's homey and rustic."

34 jw fried chicken
61 soy and ginger pork chops
110 pan-fried flounder with lemon butter sauce
189 baked rigatoni with eggplant, tomatoes and ricotta

kuniko yagi

Hinoki & the Bird, Los Angeles
hinokiandthebird.com

pro cooking Yagi's spare small plates, such as black cod scented with cedar smoke, are influenced by the techniques and clean flavors of her native Japan.

home cooking Yagi uses umami bombs like jarred chile-bean paste and soy sauce to create fast, deep flavors. "Soy sauce goes with everything!" she says.

40 chicken hot pot
56 grilled pork chops with ginger sauce
74 mapo tofu
112 seared sole with lime sauce

ricardo zarate

Mo-Chica, Los Angeles
chefzarate.com

pro cooking Zarate fuses the Peruvian food he grew up with in Lima and the Japanese technique he learned at hibachi restaurants.

home cooking At home, Zarate riffs on dishes from his childhood, using traditional Peruvian ingredients like quinoa and untraditional ones like feta cheese.

46 peruvian-style arroz con pollo
128 quinoa-crusted salmon with spicy orange-miso sauce
149 peruvian seafood and rice stew
186 peruvian-style pasta bolognese

andrew zimmern

AZ Canteen, Minneapolis
andrewzimmern.com

pro cooking On *Bizarre Foods*, Zimmern travels the world in search of the most unusual dishes—curried iguana, for instance. From his Minneapolis food truck, he serves the kind of food Americans love: hot dogs, barbecue pork and sliders.

home cooking "Many people think they're too time-poor to prepare meals at home," Zimmern says. "But cooking at home is a joy. It's a way to perpetuate all the best things about our humanity."

67 sautéed pork tenderloin with apricots and mustard
116 sea bass piccata with fried capers and leeks
182 spaghetti with veal meatballs
221 roasted peach cobbler with vanilla ice cream and balsamic syrup

weeknight WINES

These versatile bottles are perfect for weeknight drinking.

Under $15

A little adventurousness with wines in this price range really pays off. More often than not, you'll get a better bottle of wine than if you stick with familiar grapes like Chardonnay and Cabernet.

Cava

Super-dry, refreshing cavas from the Penedès region of Spain (just west of Barcelona) are great, affordable sparkling wines. They're made with indigenous Spanish grape varieties using the traditional Champagne method.
Producers to look for: Juvé y Camps, Pere Ventura, Castillo Perelada

South African Chenin Blanc

Although Chenin is native to France's Loire Valley, there's almost twice as much of it planted in South Africa. While French versions can often be a bit sweet, South African Chenin Blancs never are; fruity and full-bodied, they're wonderful with seafood and spicy dishes.
Producers to look for: Indaba, Mulderbosch, Badenhorst Secateurs

Grüner Veltliner

If you love Pinot Grigio or Sauvignon Blanc, you will feel the same way about Grüner Veltliners from Austria. They're lively, citrusy and extraordinary with food, especially vegetables and fish.
Producers to look for: Huber, Schloss Gobelsburg, Fred Loimer

Spanish Rosados

Hot-pink rosés from Spain's Rioja region are vibrant and light enough for white wine devotees and intensely fruity and bold enough for red wine drinkers.
Producers to look for: Muga, Conde de Valdemar, Cune

Côtes du Rhône

Reds from the Châteauneuf-du-Pape and Cornas regions in France's Rhône Valley are very pricey and need to age before they're ready to drink. However, most of the best producers also make affordable, blended Côtes du Rhône from vineyards in outlying areas. Have them with chicken, meat or pasta with tomato sauce.
Producers to look for: M. Chapoutier, Delas Freres, Domaine Pélaquié

Portuguese Reds

For a long time, Portugal was known only for port, but that's changing. Now, producers throughout the country are turning out stunning dry red wines that can range from lively and fruity to spicy and structured. All are outstanding with grilled meats and roasts.
Producers to look for: Álvaro Castro, Prazo de Roriz, Periquita

Over $15

Even for weeknights, it's worth spending a little more on these popular, easy-to-find, easy-to-drink varieties.

California Sparkling Wines
Because California is much warmer than Champagne, its grapes ripen quicker. The result is weightier sparkling wines that go incredibly well with food.
Producers to look for: Gloria Ferrer, Scharffenberger Cellars, Domaine Carneros

Chablis
The beauty of Chablis is that it balances remarkable acidity with body. It can go with almost any dish, from vegetables to lighter meats.
Producers to look for: William Fevre, Jean-Marc Brocard, Joseph Drouhin

New Zealand Sauvignon Blanc
New Zealand built its wine industry on Sauvignon Blanc. These herbal, citrusy wines are fantastic on their own or with vegetables and seafood.
Producers to look for: Cloudy Bay, Huia, Dog Point

Southern French Rosés
Sales of Provençal rosés have skyrocketed in the past five years, and prices are rising along with their popularity. Seek out rosés from the Languedoc, southern Rhône and Côtes de Provence: They're just as food-friendly as Provençal wines but tend to be more affordable.
Producers to look for: Domaine de Fontsainte, Domaine Sainte Lucie, Château Peyrassol

Oregon Pinot Noir
Oregon is basically synonymous with Pinot Noir; the past couple of vintages have been exceptional. These Pinots have sweet fruit and spice and are often less costly than their counterparts from California and Burgundy.
Producers to look for: Benton-Lane, Elk Cove, Chehalem

Argentinean Malbec
Malbec, a terrifically fresh, robust red, is one of the fastest-growing varieties in the US, and the wines just keep getting better and better.
Producers to look for: Catena Zapata, Pulenta Estate, Susana Balbo

You should always have good wine on hand. That way, if your dinner doesn't work out, you can at least have a glass of wine. —Alex Guarnaschelli

chicken

21 herb-roasted spatchcock chicken

22 crisp pan-roasted chicken with anchovies, capers and lemon

25 butcher shop chicken

26 crunchy baked chicken thighs with grainy mustard and garlic

29 grilled chicken with miso-basil marinade

31 crispy chicken cutlets with swiss chard

32 flash-fried chicken carnitas

← pictured   34 **jw fried chicken**

37 chipotle-braised chicken thighs with poached eggs

38 tangy chicken adobo

40 chicken hot pot

43 beer-braised chicken wings with clams and chickpeas

↓ pictured   44 **turmeric chicken and rice**

46 peruvian-style arroz con pollo

49 healthy chicken jambalaya

50 thai chicken soup

53 roast chicken panzanella

SUPER *quick* PREP

TYLER FLORENCE

herb-roasted spatchcock chicken

Active **10 min**; Total **1 hr**; Serves **4**

One 4-pound chicken
1 tablespoon olive oil
1 tablespoon chopped oregano
1 tablespoon chopped thyme
2 teaspoons chopped rosemary
Salt and freshly ground pepper
4 garlic cloves, crushed

Chef Tyler Florence of Wayfare Tavern in San Francisco gets as much crispiness as possible when roasting chicken by spatchcocking, or butterflying—removing the backbone and flattening the bird so that more of the skin is exposed to direct heat. (Your butcher can do this for you.) He serves his kale Caesar (page 154) alongside, tossing the caramelized roasted garlic from the chicken into the salad.

1. Preheat the oven to 400°. Using poultry shears, cut along each side of the chicken backbone and remove it. Turn the chicken breast side up and press on the breastbone to flatten the chicken. Rub the chicken all over with the olive oil, oregano, thyme and rosemary. Generously season with salt and pepper.

2. Transfer the chicken to a large rimmed baking sheet, skin side up, and tuck the garlic underneath it. Roast for 45 minutes, until the skin is browned and an instant-read thermometer inserted in an inner thigh registers 160°. Transfer the chicken to a cutting board and let rest for 10 minutes before serving.

CHRIS COSENTINO

crisp pan-roasted chicken with anchovies, capers and lemon

Active **15 min;** Total **45 min;** Serves **4**

One 4¼-pound chicken

Kosher salt and freshly ground pepper

2 **tablespoons extra-virgin olive oil**

1 **cup flat-leaf parsley leaves**

2 **tablespoons drained capers**

2 **garlic cloves, crushed**

½ **cup chicken stock or low-sodium broth**

¼ **cup fresh lemon juice**

12 **white anchovy fillets (*alici* or *boquerones*)**

Weighting down a butterflied chicken with a heavy pan makes it cook much faster; pressing the chicken into the hot skillet also yields crisp, crackling skin. Chef Chris Cosentino of San Francisco's Porcellino finishes the dish with a quick pan sauce of anchovies and capers, two of his favorite pantry items.

1. Preheat the oven to 425°. Using poultry shears, cut along each side of the chicken backbone and remove it. Turn the chicken breast side up and press on the breastbone to flatten the chicken. (Alternatively, ask your butcher to do this for you.) Season with salt and pepper.

2. Heat a large ovenproof skillet over moderately high heat. Add the olive oil, then add the chicken, breast side down. Place another heavy pan or pot on top of the chicken and press down firmly. Reduce the heat to moderate and cook until the skin is browned, about 5 minutes.

3. Remove the top pan and turn the chicken over. Transfer the skillet to the oven and roast the chicken for 25 minutes, until an instant-read thermometer inserted in an inner thigh registers 160°. Transfer the chicken to a platter and let rest for 10 minutes.

4. Set the hot skillet over high heat; add the parsley, capers and garlic and cook for 30 seconds, until sizzling. Add the chicken stock and lemon juice and cook, stirring and scraping up any browned bits, until the sauce has reduced by half. Stir in the anchovies and pour the sauce over the chicken.

SERVE WITH Arugula salad and lemon wedges.

butcher shop chicken

Active **25 min**; Total **45 min**; Serves **4**

- 2 shallots, chopped
- 1 carrot, chopped
- 1 celery rib, chopped
- 2 bone-in, skin-on chicken breast halves
- 2 whole chicken legs
- 3 tablespoons extra-virgin olive oil
- Salt and freshly ground black pepper
- 1½ teaspoons finely chopped rosemary
- 3 tablespoons finely chopped basil
- 1 teaspoon finely chopped thyme
- 1 garlic clove, thinly sliced
- 2 pints grape tomatoes, halved
- 1 teaspoon sherry vinegar
- ¼ teaspoon crushed red pepper

This recipe from chef John Besh of August in New Orleans gives you everything you want in a roast chicken—juicy white and dark meat—without the trouble of carving at the table. He serves the chicken pieces with a warm, basil-flecked tomato salad.

1. Preheat the oven to 450°. In a small roasting pan, scatter the shallots, carrot and celery in an even layer.

2. Rub the chicken with 2 tablespoons of the olive oil, then generously season with salt and black pepper. Arrange the chicken skin side up on top of the vegetables in the pan and sprinkle with the rosemary, 1 tablespoon of the basil and ½ teaspoon of the thyme.

3. Roast the chicken for 35 minutes, until an instant-read thermometer inserted in an inner thigh registers 165°. The skin should be golden brown and the juices should run clear.

4. Meanwhile, in a small skillet, heat the remaining 1 tablespoon of olive oil over moderately high heat. Add the garlic and cook, stirring, for 45 seconds, until golden brown. Add the tomatoes, vinegar and red pepper; season with salt. Cook, stirring frequently, until the tomatoes are softened, about 3 minutes. Transfer to a serving bowl, stir in the remaining 2 tablespoons of basil and ½ teaspoon of thyme and season with salt and black pepper. Serve the tomatoes with the roast chicken and vegetables.

crunchy baked chicken thighs with grainy mustard and garlic

Active **15 min**; Total **45 min**; Serves **4 to 6**

- 3 **tablespoons grainy mustard**
- 1 **tablespoon Dijon mustard**
- 1 **tablespoon Worcestershire sauce**
- 1 **garlic clove, finely grated**
- ½ **teaspoon cayenne pepper**
- ¾ **cup plain dried bread crumbs**
- 3 **tablespoons unsalted butter, melted**
- 2 **tablespoons finely chopped flat-leaf parsley**
- 1 **teaspoon finely grated lemon zest**
- 6 **skinless, boneless chicken thighs (2 pounds)**

  Kosher salt and freshly ground black pepper

  Lemon wedges, for serving

"I'm a sucker for mustard with chicken," says Alex Guarnaschelli, chef at Butter in Manhattan. The mustard in this recipe not only helps the bread crumbs adhere to the chicken, it adds fast flavor. "Double the recipe," she insists. "I love the leftovers in a sandwich."

1. Preheat the oven to 450°. Set a wire rack on a rimmed baking sheet.

2. In a large bowl, mix the mustards with the Worcestershire sauce, garlic and cayenne. In a large, shallow dish, toss the bread crumbs with the butter, parsley and lemon zest.

3. Season the chicken with salt and black pepper. Add to the mustard mixture and turn to coat. Dredge the skinned side of 1 chicken thigh in the bread crumb mixture and transfer to the rack, crumb side up. Repeat with the remaining chicken.

4. Transfer the chicken to the oven and bake for 30 minutes, until the crumbs are golden brown and the chicken is cooked through. Serve with lemon wedges.

TIM BYRES

grilled chicken with miso-basil marinade

Active **20 min;** Total **50 min;** Serves **4**

1½ cups basil leaves

5 garlic cloves, coarsely chopped

One 1-inch piece of fresh ginger, peeled and coarsely chopped

1 shallot, coarsely chopped

½ jalapeño, seeded and coarsely chopped

1 teaspoon finely grated lime zest

2 tablespoons fresh lime juice

2 tablespoons white wine

¼ cup *shiro* (white) miso

1 tablespoon honey

2 tablespoons extra-virgin olive oil

4 bone-in, skin-on chicken breast halves

Salt

Chef Tim Byres of Smoke in Dallas marinates chicken breasts in a zippy blend of miso, basil, jalapeño and lime juice. (It's also great on pork.) The chicken is wonderful grilled; alternatively, it can be roasted at 450° for about 40 minutes.

1. In a blender, puree the basil, garlic, ginger, shallot, jalapeño, lime zest and juice and wine until smooth. Add the miso and honey and puree until very smooth. With the machine on, add the olive oil.

2. In a large glass dish, generously season the chicken with salt and coat with the marinade. Let stand for at least 15 minutes or up to 8 hours.

3. Light a grill. Wipe the marinade off the chicken, season with salt and grill skin side down over moderately high heat until the chicken releases easily from the grill, about 8 minutes. Turn and grill until the chicken is white throughout, 10 to 12 minutes longer, then serve.

MAKE AHEAD The marinade can be refrigerated for up to 3 days.

"

Feel free to improvise the breading for this chicken. Triscuits, cornflakes, Grape-Nuts, panko—these all make great crusts.

"

crispy chicken cutlets with swiss chard

Active **15 min**; Total **50 min**; Serves **4**

- **2 tablespoons olive oil, plus more for brushing**
- **20 shredded-wheat crackers, such as Triscuits**
- **2½ cups cornflakes**
- **2 tablespoons sesame seeds**
- **½ teaspoon garlic powder**
- **Freshly ground black pepper**
- **1 cup plain low-fat yogurt**
- **1 tablespoon Dijon mustard**
- **Kosher salt**
- **4 skinless, boneless chicken thighs (1½ pounds)**
- **2 garlic cloves, sliced**
- **Pinch of crushed red pepper**
- **2 bunches of Swiss chard (about 2½ pounds), stems removed and leaves torn**
- **Lemon wedges, mustard and/or hot sauce, for serving**

"My family loves chicken *tonkatsu* at Japanese restaurants," says Matt Jennings. "This version is baked, not fried, and no one can tell the difference." He and his wife, Kate, co-chefs at the forthcoming Townsman in Boston, use a blend of finely ground cornflakes and Triscuits to make the crunchiest crust.

1. Preheat the oven to 375°. Brush a large baking sheet with olive oil.

2. In a food processor, pulse the crackers into coarse crumbs. Add the cornflakes and pulse until finely ground; transfer to a wide, shallow bowl. Stir in the sesame seeds, garlic powder and ½ teaspoon of black pepper. In another wide, shallow bowl, whisk the yogurt with the mustard and ½ teaspoon of salt until smooth.

3. Dredge 1 chicken thigh in the yogurt mixture, allowing the excess to drip back into the bowl, then coat the chicken with the cracker mixture, pressing to help the crumbs adhere. Transfer the chicken to the prepared baking sheet. Repeat with the remaining chicken. Bake for about 40 minutes, until the chicken is golden and cooked through.

4. Meanwhile, in a large, deep skillet, heat the 2 tablespoons of olive oil. Add the garlic and crushed red pepper and cook over moderately high heat until the garlic is softened, about 30 seconds. Add the chard and cook, stirring, until tender but still bright green, about 5 minutes. Season with salt and black pepper. Transfer the chard to plates along with the chicken and serve with lemon wedges, mustard and/or hot sauce.

flash-fried chicken carnitas

Total **25 min;** Serves **4**

- ½ small red onion, thinly sliced
  Finely grated zest of 1 lime
- ½ cup fresh lime juice
  Salt
- 1 pound skinless, boneless chicken thighs, cut into 1½-inch pieces
- 3 tablespoons adobo seasoning (see Note)
- ¾ cup whole-wheat flour
- ¼ cup fine yellow cornmeal
- 2 tablespoons sweet paprika
- 2 large egg whites
- 6 cups plus 2 tablespoons vegetable oil
- ½ head of iceberg lettuce, thinly sliced
- 1 cup coarsely chopped cilantro
- 1 cup cherry tomatoes (about 5 ounces), halved
- 1 jalapeño, thinly sliced
  Freshly ground pepper
- 1 avocado, cut into wedges
  Lime wedges, for serving

Chef and weight-loss guru Rocco DiSpirito is not ashamed to admit that he uses the microwave for the healthy dish here. He zaps chicken thighs before frying them so they spend less time in oil.

1. In a small bowl, combine the onion with the lime zest, lime juice and a small pinch of salt; let stand for 15 minutes. Drain the onion; reserve the onion and lime juice separately.

2. Meanwhile, sprinkle the chicken with ½ tablespoon of the adobo seasoning and arrange in a single layer on a microwave-safe plate. Microwave the chicken on high power in 2-minute intervals, turning once, until just cooked through, about 7 minutes. Let cool slightly.

3. In a wide, shallow bowl, whisk the flour with the cornmeal, paprika and the remaining 2½ tablespoons of adobo seasoning. In a medium bowl, whisk the egg whites until foamy, about 1 minute. Dip the chicken pieces in the egg whites, letting the excess drip back into the bowl, then dredge them in the flour mixture; tap off any excess.

4. In a large saucepan, heat 6 cups of the oil to 400°. Fry the coated chicken pieces in 2 batches until golden brown, about 12 seconds per batch. Transfer the fried chicken to a paper towel–lined plate and season with salt and pepper.

5. In a large bowl, toss the lettuce with the cilantro, tomatoes, jalapeño, the reserved onion, 3 tablespoons of the reserved lime juice and the remaining 2 tablespoons of oil; season with salt and pepper. Serve the fried chicken with the salad, avocado and lime wedges.

NOTE The Latin spice blend adobo, with garlic, oregano, pepper and turmeric, is available at many supermarkets.

JONATHAN WAXMAN

jw fried chicken

Total **45 min;** Serves **4**

½ teaspoon crushed red pepper

½ teaspoon ground ginger

   Kosher salt and freshly ground black pepper

   One 3½-pound chicken, cut into 2 drumsticks, 2 thighs, 4 wing pieces and 6 breast pieces

1 **quart vegetable or canola oil**

2 **cups all-purpose flour**

1 **cup buttermilk**

1 **cup fine yellow cornmeal**

"There will be a chicken on my headstone, I'm so well-known for it," says chef Jonathan Waxman of Barbuto in Manhattan. For his signature fried chicken, he dips pieces in buttermilk, then dredges them in fine cornmeal to achieve a supercrunchy crust.

1. Preheat the oven to 325°. In a small bowl, combine the crushed red pepper and ginger with ½ teaspoon each of salt and black pepper. In a large bowl, coat the chicken pieces with the dry rub.

2. In a 12-inch cast-iron skillet, heat the oil to 350°. Place 1 cup of the flour and the buttermilk in 2 separate medium bowls. In a large bowl, whisk the remaining 1 cup of flour with the cornmeal and season with salt. Dredge the chicken pieces in the flour, shaking off the excess, then dip them in the buttermilk and dredge in the cornmeal mixture. Fry half of the chicken pieces, turning occasionally, until deep golden and cooked through, about 15 minutes. Transfer the fried chicken to a baking sheet and keep warm in the oven while you fry the rest. Drain on paper towels or butcher paper before serving.

JENN LOUIS

chipotle-braised chicken thighs with poached eggs

Active **25 min**; Total **1 hr**; Serves **6**

- **One 28-ounce can tomato puree**
- 2 **cups chicken stock or low-sodium broth**
- 4 **chipotle chiles in adobo**
- 1 **large white onion, cut in sixths**
- 2 **garlic cloves, sliced**
- 1 **tablespoon ground cumin**
- 1 **tablespoon ground coriander**
- 2 **tablespoons vegetable oil**
- 6 **skinless, boneless chicken thighs (about 2½ pounds)**
- **Salt**
- **One 14-ounce can pinto beans, drained and rinsed**
- **6 large eggs**
- **Toppings: Mexican *crema* or sour cream, crumbled Cotija cheese, sliced avocado and chopped jalapeños, cilantro and onion**
- **Warm corn tortillas and lime wedges, for serving**

Jenn Louis, chef at Lincoln Restaurant in Portland, Oregon, grew up three hours from Mexico, a little east of Los Angeles. Today, she often looks south of the border for dinner inspiration. Here she braises chicken thighs and poaches eggs in a smoky tomato sauce reminiscent of Mexican *tinga*.

1. Preheat the oven to 425°. In a blender, combine the tomato puree, chicken stock, chipotles, onion, garlic, cumin and coriander and puree until smooth.

2. In a large enameled cast-iron casserole or Dutch oven, heat the oil. Season the chicken with salt, add to the casserole and cook over high heat, turning once, until golden, about 8 minutes. Transfer the chicken to a plate. Drain off the fat, leaving just enough to coat the bottom of the casserole.

3. Add the tomato sauce to the casserole and bring to a simmer, scraping up any browned bits from the bottom. Season with salt. Nestle the chicken thighs in the sauce and bake for about 20 minutes, until cooked through. Stir in the pinto beans, then crack the eggs into the sauce, spacing them evenly. Bake for about 5 minutes longer, until the egg whites are set and the yolks are still runny. Drizzle *crema* on top and sprinkle with the remaining toppings. Serve straight from the casserole with corn tortillas and lime wedges.

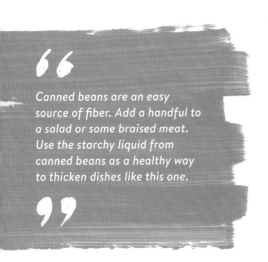

> Canned beans are an easy source of fiber. Add a handful to a salad or some braised meat. Use the starchy liquid from canned beans as a healthy way to thicken dishes like this one.

double and FREEZE

tangy chicken adobo

Total **45 min;** Serves **4**

- ¼ cup canola oil
- 1 large onion, diced
- 20 garlic cloves, coarsely chopped
  Salt
- 2 cups chicken stock or low-sodium broth
- 1 cup apple cider vinegar
- ½ cup soy sauce
- 10 fresh or dried bay leaves
- 1 teaspoon freshly ground pepper
- 2 teaspoons cornstarch stirred with 2 teaspoons water

  One 3½-pound chicken, cut into 12 pieces (breasts halved, wings separated from drumettes)

  Steamed white rice, for serving

"My wife, Meshelle, is Filipino, and her grandma is always cooking food for us," says Cathal Armstrong, chef at Restaurant Eve in Alexandria, Virginia. His version of this quintessential Filipino dish is extra-tangy thanks to the generous amount of cider vinegar. To ensure that all the chicken pieces finish cooking at the same time, halve each breast and separate the wings from the drumettes.

1. In a large skillet, heat 3 tablespoons of the oil over moderately high heat. Add the onion and garlic, season with salt and cook, stirring occasionally, until the onion is softened, about 12 minutes. Add the stock, vinegar, soy sauce, bay leaves and pepper and bring to a boil over high heat. Stir in the cornstarch slurry and simmer the sauce for 1 minute.

2. Meanwhile, in another large skillet, heat the remaining 1 tablespoon of oil over moderately high heat. Season the chicken with salt and cook skin side down, turning once, until browned, about 8 minutes. Add the chicken to the sauce, cover partially and simmer over moderately low heat, turning the chicken once, until cooked through, about 20 minutes. Discard the bay leaves and serve with rice.

chicken hot pot

Active **20 min**; Total **35 min**; Serves **4**

- **4** chicken drumsticks (1 pound)
- ½ teaspoon kosher salt
- ½ cup dark soy sauce
- **2** tablespoons fresh lemon juice
- **2** tablespoons unseasoned rice vinegar
- **3** cups thinly sliced seasonal vegetables, such as carrots, parsnips and leafy greens

  One 3-inch piece of daikon radish, peeled and grated

  One 2-inch piece of fresh ginger, peeled and grated

  Togarashi, for serving (see Note)
- **12** ounces cooked udon, soba or somen noodles or brown rice, for serving

double and FREEZE

This recipe from chef Kuniko Yagi of L.A.'s Hinoki & the Bird was inspired by Japanese *nabemono,* a pot of broth simmering on the table over a portable burner. People serve themselves, adding accompaniments like greens and daikon radish presented alongside. For extra richness, pour in a whisked egg; it will "feather" like egg drop soup.

1. In a large saucepan, cover the chicken with 8 cups of water (it should come two-thirds of the way up the side of the pan) and bring to a boil over high heat. Add the salt, then reduce the heat to moderately low and simmer gently for 20 minutes, skimming the foam occasionally.

2. Meanwhile, in a small saucepan, bring the soy sauce, lemon juice and vinegar to a simmer over high heat. Remove the *ponzu* sauce from the heat.

3. Transfer the chicken to a plate. Add any root vegetables to the simmering broth and cook until tender, about 5 minutes. Using a slotted spoon, transfer the vegetables to 4 bowls. Pull the chicken meat into large pieces, discard the skin and bones and add the chicken to the bowls.

4. Add any leafy greens to the simmering broth and cook until just wilted and bright green, about 1 minute. Transfer the greens to the bowls and add ½ cup of broth to each. (Keep the remaining broth simmering in the saucepan.) Season each serving with some of the daikon, ginger, *togarashi* and *ponzu* sauce and serve.

5. When everyone has finished eating the chicken and vegetables, stir the noodles into the simmering broth until hot, then divide the noodles and broth among the bowls, season with more daikon, ginger, *togarashi* and *ponzu* sauce and serve.

NOTE *Togarashi,* a Japanese blend of chiles and sesame seeds, is available at Asian markets.

MAKE AHEAD The *ponzu* sauce can be refrigerated for up to 3 days.

JAMIE BISSONNETTE

beer-braised chicken wings with clams and chickpeas

Total **40 min**; Serves **4**

- **1** **pound chicken wings**
- **1** **tablespoon Old Bay seasoning**
  Kosher salt and freshly ground pepper
- **4** **tablespoons unsalted butter**
- **1** **medium onion, finely chopped**
- **5** **garlic cloves, minced**
- **1** **fresh bay leaf**
- **1** **tablespoon tomato paste**
- **12** **littleneck clams, scrubbed**
- **1** **cup beer, such as lager**
- **2** **cups chicken stock or low-sodium broth**
  One 15-ounce can chickpeas, drained and rinsed
- **2** **tablespoons chopped flat-leaf parsley**

This dish was a "wicked lucky success" for chef Jamie Bissonnette of Toro in Boston and Manhattan. Inspired by beer-steamed clams, he took a pound of chicken wings out of the fridge and came up with this hybrid recipe when he had some unexpected dinner guests one evening.

1. Preheat the oven to 350°. On a rimmed baking sheet, toss the chicken wings with the Old Bay and season with salt and pepper. Spread out the wings and roast for 10 minutes, until the skin looks tight.

2. Meanwhile, in a large, deep skillet, melt the butter over moderate heat. Add the onion, garlic, bay leaf and a pinch each of salt and pepper. Cook, stirring occasionally, until the onion is softened but not browned, about 10 minutes.

3. Add the tomato paste and chicken wings to the skillet and stir until the wings are well coated, then stir in the clams. Add the beer and bring to a boil over high heat. Boil for 3 minutes, then add the stock and chickpeas. Season with salt and pepper. Cook, stirring occasionally, until the clams open, 5 to 10 minutes; as they open, transfer them to a serving bowl. Discard any clams that do not open. Stir the parsley into the skillet, then spoon the chicken wings and broth over the clams.

SERVE WITH Grilled bread.

EDWARD LEE

turmeric chicken and rice

Active **35 min**; Total **1 hr 10 min**
Serves **4**

One 4½-pound chicken, cut into 8 pieces

Salt and freshly ground pepper

2 tablespoons unsalted butter

1½ teaspoons ground turmeric

1 small onion, chopped

1 tablespoon finely chopped peeled fresh ginger

4 garlic cloves, minced

2 plum tomatoes, chopped

2 teaspoons curry powder

½ teaspoon cinnamon

½ teaspoon ground cumin

2 cups jasmine rice

3 bay leaves

1½ tablespoons Asian fish sauce

3 cups chicken stock or low-sodium broth

Plain whole-milk yogurt, sliced cucumbers, mint leaves and lime wedges, for serving

Chef Edward Lee of 610 Magnolia in Louisville, Kentucky, takes culinary inspiration from all parts of Asia. He gives this Southeast Asian–inflected recipe a warm, complex flavor with curry powder and ginger, adding turmeric for an appealing marigold tinge. For serving, Lee says, "This is a meal that is best eaten family style, so let everyone garnish their own plate."

1. Season the chicken with salt and pepper. In a large enameled cast-iron casserole or Dutch oven, melt the butter and sprinkle with the turmeric. Add the chicken skin side down and cook over moderately high heat, turning once, until browned on both sides, about 8 minutes total. Transfer the chicken to a plate.

2. Add the onion, ginger and garlic to the casserole and cook, stirring occasionally, until starting to brown, about 5 minutes. Add the tomatoes, curry powder, cinnamon, cumin and rice and stir constantly until fragrant, about 1 minute. Return the chicken to the pot, skin side up. Add the bay leaves, fish sauce and chicken stock and bring to a boil over high heat.

3. Cover the casserole and simmer over low heat for 10 minutes. Adjust the lid to cover partially and simmer until the rice is cooked, 10 to 15 minutes longer. Remove from the heat, uncover and let stand for 5 minutes. Discard the bay leaves. Serve with yogurt, cucumbers, mint and lime wedges.

ONE-POT meal

RICARDO ZARATE

peruvian-style arroz con pollo

1¾ cups crushed saltine crackers

1½ cups whole milk

¼ cup plus 1 tablespoon canola oil

2 tablespoons minced red onion

¾ ounce ají amarillo chiles or 1 habanero chile, seeded and minced

1 ounce feta cheese, crumbled (¼ cup)

Salt and freshly ground pepper

4 skinless, boneless chicken breast halves (1½ pounds)

1 medium carrot, finely diced

4 cups cooked medium-grain white rice

3 cups chicken stock or low-sodium broth

1 cup frozen peas, thawed

1 cup cilantro, chopped

Salsa criolla (page 149), for serving

At his L.A. restaurant Paiche, Lima native Ricardo Zarate reinvents his mother's home cooking with dishes like this arroz con pollo. He tops the chicken and rice with two Peruvian-style condiments: *salsa criolla*, a fresh tomato and lime salsa; and feta *huancaina*, a creamy, spicy sauce that's typically served with cold boiled potatoes.

1. Preheat the oven to 375°. In a blender, soak the saltines in the milk.

2. Meanwhile, in a small skillet, heat 1 tablespoon of the oil over moderate heat. Add the onion and chiles and cook, stirring, until the onion is softened and golden. Transfer to the blender, add the feta and puree until smooth. Season the feta *huancaina* with salt and pepper.

3. Generously season the chicken with salt and pepper. In a large ovenproof skillet, heat 2 tablespoons of the oil over high heat. Add the chicken and cook until golden brown, 4 to 5 minutes. Turn the chicken over, transfer the skillet to the oven and roast for about 10 minutes, until just cooked through.

4. Meanwhile, in a large saucepan, heat the remaining 2 tablespoons of oil. Add the carrot, season with salt and cook over moderately high heat until softened and lightly browned, 3 to 4 minutes. Add the rice and cook, stirring, for 1 minute. Add the chicken stock and bring to a boil. Reduce the heat and simmer, stirring constantly, until the rice resembles risotto, about 5 minutes.

5. Transfer the chicken breasts to a work surface and let them rest for 5 minutes. Stir any chicken pan juices into the rice along with the peas and cilantro. Spoon the rice onto plates. Slice the chicken breasts crosswise and arrange on the rice. Serve with the feta *huancaina* and *salsa criolla*.

healthy chicken jambalaya

Active **20 min**; Total **40 min**; Serves **4**

- **1** tablespoon olive oil
- **4** skinless, boneless chicken thighs (about 1 pound), cut into 2-inch pieces
  Salt and freshly ground pepper
- **1** andouille sausage (about 3 ounces), sliced ½ inch thick
- **1** medium onion, chopped
- **1** small red bell pepper, chopped
- **2** garlic cloves, minced
- **1** teaspoon adobo seasoning
- **¼** teaspoon chipotle chile powder
- **1** cup long-grain rice
- **2** cups chicken stock or low-sodium broth
- **½** cup canned black beans, drained and rinsed

This leaner take on jambalaya features much less andouille sausage than the classic (health-conscious chef Rocco DiSpirito prefers chicken and turkey andouille). To make up for the assertively spiced meat, DiSpirito amps up the rice with chipotle chile powder and adobo seasoning, a zesty spice blend of garlic, oregano and black pepper.

1. In a large, deep skillet, heat the oil until shimmering. Season the chicken with salt and pepper and cook over moderately high heat, turning once, until browned, about 3 minutes. Transfer to a plate. Add the sausage to the skillet and cook until lightly browned on both sides, about 2 minutes. Add the sausage to the plate with the chicken.

2. Add the onion, pepper and garlic to the skillet and cook, stirring frequently, until lightly browned, about 6 minutes. Add the adobo seasoning and chile powder and cook until fragrant, about 30 seconds. Add the rice and cook, stirring constantly, until well coated and just beginning to brown, about 1 minute. Stir in the stock, black beans, chicken and sausage and bring to a boil over moderately high heat. Cover and cook over moderately low heat until the rice is tender and the chicken is cooked through, about 15 minutes. Let rest for 5 minutes, then fluff the rice with a fork and serve.

SPIKE GJERDE

thai chicken soup

Active **25 min**; Total **45 min**; Serves **4**

- 3 **quarts chicken stock or low-sodium broth**
- 1 **lemongrass stalk, cut into 4-inch lengths**
- **One 2-inch piece of fresh ginger, sliced**
- 4 **fresh Thai bird chiles**
- **Four 1-inch strips of lime zest**
- 1 **large head of cauliflower, cut into small florets**
- ½ **pound shiitake mushrooms, stemmed and caps sliced ½ inch thick**
- **One 13½-ounce can unsweetened coconut milk**
- 4 **cups shredded cooked chicken**
- 1 **cup frozen shelled edamame, thawed**
- ¾ **cup fresh lime juice (from about 5 limes)**
- ½ **cup Asian fish sauce**
- **Salt**
- ½ **cup chopped cilantro**

"My wife, Amy, has celiac disease, so at home I cook things you can have with rice instead of high-gluten carbs like pasta," says Spike Gjerde, chef at Woodberry Kitchen in Baltimore. He makes the light, tangy broth here with ginger, lime and fresh lemongrass that Amy grows in their garden.

1. In a large saucepan, combine the chicken stock, lemongrass, ginger, chiles and lime zest and bring to a boil. Simmer over moderately low heat for 10 minutes, then strain and return the broth to the saucepan. Discard the solids.

2. Add the cauliflower, shiitake and coconut milk to the broth and bring to a boil, then simmer over moderate heat until the cauliflower is crisp-tender, about 5 minutes. Add the chicken and edamame and simmer just until heated through, about 2 minutes. Stir in the lime juice and fish sauce and season with salt. Garnish with the cilantro and serve.

MAKE AHEAD The soup can be refrigerated for up to 2 days.

EVAN AND SARAH RICH

roast chicken panzanella

Active **30 min**; Total **45 min**; Serves **4**

- ¾ **pound country bread or sourdough, torn into 1-inch pieces (8 cups)**
- ¼ **cup plus 2 tablespoons extra-virgin olive oil**

  Salt and freshly ground pepper
- ½ **small red onion, chopped**
- ¼ **cup Champagne vinegar**
- ¼ **cup sherry vinegar**
- 2 **romaine hearts, torn into bite-size pieces**
- 1 **large tomato, chopped**
- 2 **Persian cucumbers, chopped**
- 1 **cup strawberries, hulled and chopped**
- 1 **cup cilantro leaves**
- 2 **tablespoons chopped dill**

  One 2½- to 3-pound rotisserie chicken, meat shredded (about 4 cups)
- ¼ **cup salted toasted pumpkin seeds**

This main-course version of bread salad, interpreted through a California lens, includes shredded rotisserie chicken, strawberries, cilantro and toasted pumpkin seeds. "My husband, Evan, and I make wild fennel levain at Rich Table, and this is a delicious way to use up day-old bread," says San Francisco chef Sarah Rich.

1. Preheat the oven to 350°. On a large rimmed baking sheet, toss the bread with 2 tablespoons of the olive oil and season with salt and pepper. Bake for 15 minutes, until golden brown and crisp. Let cool.

2. Meanwhile, in a large bowl, toss the onion with both vinegars and let stand for 10 minutes. Whisk in the remaining ¼ cup of olive oil and season with salt and pepper. Add the romaine pieces, tomato, cucumbers, strawberries, cilantro, dill, chicken and the toasted bread and toss well. Transfer the salad to a platter, sprinkle with the pumpkin seeds and serve.

pork

56 grilled pork chops with ginger sauce
58 chicken-fried pork chops
61 soy and ginger pork chops
62 pork blade steaks with sage butter sauce
64 pork and chorizo pozole
67 sautéed pork tenderloin with apricots and mustard
68 ginger-braised pork meatballs in coconut broth
← <u>pictured</u>   **70** **cheater's ramen with country ham, parmesan and egg**
73 chorizo with rice and lentils
74 mapo tofu
77 italian sausage salad

grilled pork chops with ginger sauce

Active **5 min;** Total **20 min;** Serves **4**

- 2 **tablespoons mirin**
- 2 **tablespoons sake**
- 2 **tablespoons finely chopped peeled fresh ginger**
- 2 **tablespoons soy sauce**
- ¼ **cup extra-virgin olive oil**
- **Four 10- to 12-ounce bone-in pork chops, about 1 inch thick**
- **Salt and freshly ground pepper**

Kuniko Yagi's secret ginger sauce is all-purpose: The chef at L.A.'s Hinoki & the Bird seasons everything with it—these pork chops, for starters, but also steamed eggplant and grilled bok choy.

1. Light a grill or preheat a grill pan. In a small saucepan, bring the mirin and sake to a boil and simmer for 30 seconds. Stir in the ginger, soy sauce and 2 tablespoons of the olive oil. Remove from the heat.

2. Season the pork chops with salt and pepper, rub them with the remaining 2 tablespoons of olive oil and grill over moderately high heat for about 6 minutes per side, until nicely charred outside and just pink in the center. Transfer the pork chops to plates and pour the ginger sauce on top.

SERVE WITH Steamed white rice and grilled bok choy.

MAKE AHEAD The ginger sauce can be refrigerated for up to 3 days.

JONATHON SAWYER

chicken-fried pork chops

Total **30 min;** Serves **4**

- **3** bay leaves, finely crushed
- **1** tablespoon sweet paprika
- **1** tablespoon sugar
- **2** teaspoons freshly ground pepper
- **1** teaspoon dried oregano
  Salt
- **4** boneless 1-inch-thick pork chops
- **2** cups all-purpose flour
- **2** cups buttermilk
- **2** tablespoons malt vinegar
- **2** tablespoons *sambal oelek* or other Asian chile sauce
- **1** tablespoon Asian fish sauce
- **1** cup vegetable oil

Chef Jonathon Sawyer of Cleveland's Greenhouse Tavern believes that you can chicken-fry lots of things, like these pork chops: He dips boneless chops in a buttermilk mixture, dredges them in seasoned flour, then fries them until they're crisp and juicy.

1. In a wide, shallow bowl, combine the crushed bay leaves with the paprika, sugar, pepper, oregano and 1 tablespoon of salt. Generously season the pork chops with the spice mix and transfer them to a plate. Stir the flour into the remaining spice mix.

2. In another wide, shallow bowl, whisk the buttermilk with the vinegar, *sambal* and fish sauce. Dip the seasoned pork chops in the buttermilk mixture, allowing the excess to drip back into the bowl, then dredge them in the flour mixture, pressing to help it adhere.

3. In a large cast-iron skillet, heat the vegetable oil until shimmering. Working in 2 batches, fry the chops over moderate heat, turning once, until golden and crispy, about 3 minutes per side. Drain on paper towels and season lightly with salt.

SERVE WITH Lemon wedges and mixed salad.

Pork chops can be so dry! This soy and ginger sauce keeps them moist and adds a great dimension of flavor while still leaving the essential porky taste.

JONATHAN WAXMAN

soy and ginger pork chops

Total **25 min;** Serves **4**

Olive oil, for greasing

1 whole star anise pod

½ teaspoon ground cumin

½ teaspoon ground coriander

½ teaspoon ground fennel

½ teaspoon smoked paprika

½ teaspoon cinnamon

Kosher salt and freshly ground pepper

Four 8-ounce bone-in pork chops, about ½ inch thick

¼ cup soy sauce

2 tablespoons unseasoned rice vinegar

2 tablespoons toasted sesame oil

1 tablespoon finely grated peeled fresh ginger

4 tablespoons unsalted butter, cut into tablespoons

Cilantro leaves, for garnish

"The broiler is an underutilized part of the oven," observes Jonathan Waxman, chef at Barbuto in Manhattan. Here, he broils pork chops for just a few minutes on each side, then spoons a tangy soy-ginger sauce on top.

1. Preheat the broiler. Lightly grease a medium roasting pan with olive oil.

2. In a spice grinder, finely grind the star anise pod. Transfer to a small bowl and stir in the cumin, coriander, fennel, paprika, cinnamon and ½ teaspoon each of salt and pepper. Rub the spice mix all over the pork chops. Set the chops in the roasting pan and broil 6 inches from the heat until golden and cooked through, 4 to 5 minutes per side. Transfer the pork chops to plates.

3. Add the soy sauce, vinegar, sesame oil and ginger to the roasting pan and simmer over moderate heat for 2 minutes, stirring and scraping up any browned bits with a wooden spoon. Whisk in the butter.

4. Spoon the soy-ginger sauce over the pork chops and garnish with cilantro.

SERVE WITH Sautéed spinach.

SUPER *quick* PREP

pork blade steaks with sage butter sauce

Total **15 min;** Serves **4**

Two 15-ounce pork blade steaks, about 1 inch thick

Kosher salt and freshly ground pepper

6 **tablespoons unsalted butter, at room temperature**

¾ **cup sage leaves, chopped**

¼ **cup plus 2 tablespoons apple cider vinegar**

Chef Chris Cosentino of Porcellino in San Francisco loves pork blade steak: It's well marbled, intensely flavorful and nicely chewy, plus it cooks quickly in a skillet. Also called pork steak or pork shoulder steak, it's an inexpensive cut from the shoulder that contains the blade bone.

1. Generously season the pork steaks with salt and pepper. Heat a large, heavy skillet over moderately high heat. Add 3 tablespoons of the butter and swirl to coat the bottom of the skillet, then add the steaks. Cook, turning once, until browned and just cooked through, about 10 minutes. Transfer the steaks to a platter.

2. Add the sage leaves to the skillet and cook over moderately high heat, stirring, until crisp, about 30 seconds. Add the vinegar and bring to a boil, stirring and scraping up the browned bits from the bottom of the skillet. Simmer until reduced by half. Remove the skillet from the heat and stir in the remaining 3 tablespoons of butter, 1 tablespoon at a time, until the sauce is creamy; season with salt and pepper. Slice the steaks and spoon the sauce on top.

SERVE WITH Endive salad with wedges of tart apple.

double and FREEZE

pork and chorizo pozole

Active **25 min**; Total **55 min**

Serves **6 to 8**

- ¼ cup olive oil
- 2 pounds trimmed boneless pork shoulder, cut into 1-inch cubes

  Salt and freshly ground pepper
- 1 large white onion, quartered
- 2 cloves
- 1 tablespoon dried oregano, preferably Mexican, plus more for garnish
- 2 bay leaves
- 2 quarts beef broth
- 1 pound tomatillos, husked and rinsed
- 4 plum tomatoes, halved
- 3 garlic cloves
- 1 ounce each of ancho and guajillo chiles, stemmed and seeded
- 1 pound fresh Mexican chorizo, casings removed

  Two 15-ounce cans white hominy, drained and rinsed

  Thinly sliced radishes, chopped onion and cilantro and lime wedges, for serving

Pozole is a slow-simmered, elaborately spiced Mexican stew made with hominy (dried corn kernels soaked in a mineral lime bath). This streamlined version from *Chopped* judge Aarón Sánchez, chef at Mestizo in Leawood, Kansas, uses two time-saving ingredients: fresh chorizo (which is already spiced) and pork cut into small, quick-cooking cubes.

1. In a large enameled cast-iron casserole, heat 2 tablespoons of the olive oil. Season the pork with salt and pepper, add to the casserole and cook over moderately high heat, stirring twice, until browned, about 8 minutes. Add 1 piece of the quartered onion, the cloves, the 1 tablespoon of oregano, the bay leaves and 6 cups of the beef broth and bring to a boil. Cover and simmer over moderately low heat until the pork is tender, about 40 minutes. Discard the bay leaves.

2. Meanwhile, heat a large cast-iron skillet. In a large bowl, toss the tomatillos, tomatoes, garlic and remaining 3 pieces of onion with 1 tablespoon of the olive oil; season with salt and pepper. Add the vegetables to the skillet and cook over moderately high heat until blistered in spots, about 10 minutes. Transfer the vegetables to a blender.

3. In the same skillet, toast the chiles over moderately high heat until slightly darkened, about 2 minutes. Add the remaining 2 cups of beef broth and bring to a simmer; cover the skillet, remove from the heat and let the chiles soften for 5 minutes. Add the chiles and broth to the blender with the vegetables and puree until smooth. Strain the vegetable-chile puree into a bowl. Wipe out the skillet.

4. Heat the remaining 1 tablespoon of olive oil in the skillet. Add the chorizo and cook over moderate heat, breaking it up with a spoon, until browned, about 5 minutes. Add the chorizo, hominy and vegetable-chile puree to the casserole and bring the pozole to a simmer. Season with salt and pepper. Garnish the pozole with radishes, onion, cilantro and oregano and serve with lime wedges.

ANDREW ZIMMERN

sautéed pork tenderloin with apricots and mustard

Total **40 min**; Serves **4**

- ½ cup all-purpose flour
- 1½ pounds pork tenderloin, sliced on the diagonal ½ inch thick
- Salt and freshly ground black pepper
- 4 tablespoons unsalted butter
- 1 medium shallot, finely chopped
- 1 parsley sprig
- 1 rosemary sprig
- 1 thyme sprig
- ¼ teaspoon crushed red pepper
- 1 cup dry white wine
- ½ cup fresh orange juice
- 2 tablespoons Dijon mustard
- 1 tablespoon brown mustard
- 1 cup cherry tomatoes, halved (6 ounces)
- ½ cup dried apricots, thinly sliced

"Pork with fruit and mustard is one of the greatest combinations," says Andrew Zimmern, host of Travel Channel's *Bizarre Foods.* He came up with this recipe as a foolproof way to "achieve it all" in a single pan.

1. Put the flour in a large bowl. Season the pork with salt and black pepper and dredge in the flour; tap off the excess. In a 12-inch skillet, melt 2 tablespoons of the butter. Add half of the pork and cook over moderately high heat until golden brown all over, about 8 minutes. Transfer to a plate and repeat with the remaining butter and pork.

2. Add the shallot, parsley, rosemary, thyme and crushed red pepper to the skillet and cook over moderate heat, stirring, until the shallot is softened, about 2 minutes. Add the wine and simmer until reduced by half, about 3 minutes. Add the orange juice, mustards, tomatoes, apricots and the pork and season with salt and black pepper. Cover and simmer until the apricots are softened and the pork is cooked through, about 10 minutes. Uncover and simmer until the sauce is slightly thickened, about 1 minute.

SERVE WITH Roasted potatoes.

JENN LOUIS

ginger-braised pork meatballs in coconut broth

Active **30 min**; Total **1 hr**; Serves **6**

MEATBALLS

- 2 **pounds ground pork**
- 2 **large eggs**
- 3 **tablespoons panko**
- 3 **tablespoons finely chopped peeled fresh ginger**
- 2 **garlic cloves, minced**
- 1 **tablespoon Asian fish sauce**
- 2 **teaspoons kosher salt**

BROTH

- **One 13½-ounce can unsweetened coconut milk**
- 2 **cups chicken stock or low-sodium broth**
- ¼ **cup thinly sliced peeled fresh ginger**
- 2 **garlic cloves, thinly sliced**
- 2 **fresh red Thai chiles, slit but kept intact, plus thinly sliced chiles for serving**
- 1 **stalk of fresh lemongrass, outer leaves removed and stalk cut into 1-inch lengths**
- **Finely grated zest and juice of ½ lime**
- 1 **tablespoon Asian fish sauce**
- 1 **teaspoon ground turmeric**
- **Sugar**
- **Kosher salt**
- **Thinly sliced mint and cilantro leaves, lime wedges and steamed jasmine rice, for serving**

Jenn Louis, chef at Lincoln Restaurant in Portland, Oregon, usually cooks at least one Asian-inspired meal a week. Here, she simmers gingery meatballs in a coconut milk–spiked chicken broth fragrant with lemongrass and lime. "This dish always makes me feel like I get a little vacation from what I normally eat at the restaurant."

1. Make the meatballs Preheat the oven to 425°. Combine all of the ingredients in a large bowl. Form the mixture into forty 1½-inch meatballs and arrange them on a large rimmed baking sheet about 1 inch apart. Bake until the meatballs are golden brown and just cooked through, about 15 minutes.

2. Meanwhile, make the broth In a large saucepan, combine the coconut milk, stock, ginger, garlic, slit chiles, lemongrass, lime zest and juice, fish sauce and turmeric. Add 1 tablespoon of sugar and season with salt. Bring to a boil over high heat, then reduce the heat so the broth is simmering. Discard the lemongrass.

3. Add the meatballs to the broth and simmer until cooked through and tender, about 15 minutes. Season the broth with more sugar, salt and lime juice if necessary. Serve with sliced herbs and Thai chiles, lime wedges and rice.

MAKE AHEAD The uncooked meatballs can be refrigerated on the baking sheet for up to 1 day.

double and FREEZE

At home, I take the time to learn from different ethnic cookbooks. It's like taking a class; I'll spend weeks at a time cooking various recipes from one book.

EDWARD LEE

cheater's ramen with country ham, parmesan and egg

Active **30 min**; Total **50 min**; Serves **4**

BROTH

- **1 tablespoon unsalted butter**
- **3 ounces country ham, prosciutto or serrano ham, coarsely chopped**
- **1 small onion, chopped**
- **3 garlic cloves, crushed**
- **One 1-inch piece of fresh ginger**
- **3 cups chicken stock or low-sodium broth**
- **2 teaspoons Asian fish sauce**
- **2 teaspoons red miso**
- **2 teaspoons soy sauce**

Making restaurant-style ramen takes days. A quick cheat is to add instant ramen noodles to chicken broth enriched with smoky country ham. Chef Edward Lee of 610 Magnolia in Louisville, Kentucky, likes springy Neoguri noodles, a type of Korean instant ramen that can be found at Asian markets.

1. Make the broth In a medium saucepan, melt the butter. Add the ham, onion, garlic and ginger and cook over moderately high heat until the onion is starting to brown, about 5 minutes. Add the stock, fish sauce, miso, soy sauce and ½ cup of water and bring to a boil. Simmer, uncovered, until the broth is flavorful, about 20 minutes. Strain the broth and discard the solids. Return the broth to the pan and keep warm.

RAMEN

- **2**   **tablespoons white vinegar**
- **4**   **large eggs**
- **8**   **ounces dried instant ramen noodles**
- **8**   **thin slices of country ham, prosciutto or serrano ham (about ½ pound)**
- **¼**   **cup Parmigiano-Reggiano cheese shavings**
- **1**   **Hass avocado, thinly sliced**
- **2**   **scallions, thinly sliced**
- **2**   **sheets of nori, quartered**

2. Meanwhile, make the ramen Bring a large, deep skillet of water to a simmer over moderate heat; add the vinegar. One at a time, break the eggs into a small bowl and slide them into the simmering water, leaving plenty of space between them. Poach the eggs until the whites are set and the yolks are still runny, about 4 minutes. Using a slotted spoon, carefully transfer the eggs to a paper towel–lined plate.

3. Bring a medium saucepan of water to a boil over high heat. Add the noodles and cook until al dente. Drain and transfer the noodles to large soup bowls. Top with the poached eggs. Ladle the hot broth on top and serve with the ham, cheese, avocado, scallions and nori.

RICK BAYLESS

chorizo with rice and lentils

Active **20 min;** Total **55 min;** Serves **4**

- **2 tablespoons plus 1 teaspoon olive oil**
- **3 scallions, white and green parts thinly sliced separately**
- **Salt**
- **⅓ cup French green (Le Puy) lentils, picked over and rinsed**
- **1 cup jasmine rice**
- **1 pound fresh Mexican chorizo**

Chef Rick Bayless of Frontera Grill in Chicago gives this simple rice and lentil dish a flavor boost with Mexican chorizo, a fresh pork sausage that's liberally seasoned with spices, chiles and vinegar. Unlike Spanish chorizo, which is dried and cured, the Mexican variety must be cooked before serving.

1. In a large saucepan, heat 2 tablespoons of the oil. Add the scallion whites and cook over moderate heat until softened, about 2 minutes; season with salt. Add the lentils and ¾ cup of water and bring to a boil. Cover and cook over low heat until the lentils are almost tender and the pan is nearly dry, about 25 minutes.

2. Add the rice and 2 cups of water to the saucepan and bring to a boil. Cover and cook over low heat until the lentils are tender, about 15 minutes. Remove from the heat and let stand for 5 minutes. Fluff the rice, season with salt and cover.

3. Meanwhile, in a large nonstick skillet, heat the remaining 1 teaspoon of oil. Add the chorizo and cook, turning occasionally, until firm, browned and cooked through, about 12 minutes. Slice the chorizo and serve with the rice and lentils, garnished with the scallion greens.

SUPER quick PREP

KUNIKO YAGI

mapo tofu

Total **15 min;** Serves **4**

- 1 teaspoon canola oil
- ½ pound ground pork
- ½ pound ground beef chuck (85 percent lean)
- Salt
- 2 tablespoons chile-bean sauce, preferably *toban djan*
- 2 tablespoons hoisin sauce or *tenmenjan* (soybean paste)
- 1 tablespoon soy sauce
- One 14-ounce package soft tofu, finely diced
- 1½ teaspoons cornstarch
- 3 scallions, finely chopped
- Steamed white rice, for serving

"I'm sure Chinese people wouldn't call this mapo tofu!" says Kuniko Yagi about her inauthentic meat-heavy version. Jarred *toban djan* gives this dish from the chef at L.A.'s Hinoki & the Bird its signature heat and deeply savory flavor, but any other chile-bean sauce is a fine substitute.

1. Heat a large skillet until hot. Add the oil, then the pork and beef. Season with salt and cook over high heat, stirring and breaking up the meat, until crumbly and lightly browned, about 3 minutes.

2. Stir in the chile-bean sauce, hoisin and soy sauce and cook, stirring, for 3 minutes. Gently fold in the tofu. In a small bowl, whisk the cornstarch into ½ cup of water. Add to the skillet and simmer until the sauce thickens, 2 minutes. Stir in the scallions and serve with rice.

NOTE *Toban djan* and *tenmenjan* are available at Asian food markets.

italian sausage salad

Total **40 min;** Serves **4**

- ⅓ cup red wine vinegar
- ⅓ cup canola oil
- 1 teaspoon dried oregano, preferably Mexican
- 1 teaspoon sugar
- 1 teaspoon garlic powder

  Pinch of crushed red pepper

  Kosher salt and freshly ground black pepper
- 2 medium carrots, thinly sliced
- 1 large seedless cucumber, cut into ½-inch chunks
- 1 pound hot or sweet Italian sausages
- 1 small head of iceberg lettuce, chopped (8 cups)
- 16 peperoncini—stemmed, seeded and sliced (1 cup)

As an homage to the salads of his youth, marinated in bottled Italian dressing, Jamie Bissonnette developed this "grown-up" version. The chef at Toro in Boston and New York City makes his own iceberg lettuce salad with grilled Italian sausage and vegetables marinated in a red wine vinaigrette.

1. Preheat a grill pan. In a very large bowl, whisk the vinegar, oil, oregano, sugar, garlic powder, red pepper and a pinch each of salt and black pepper. Stir in the carrots and cucumber and let stand for at least 30 minutes.

2. Meanwhile, grill the sausages over moderately low heat for about 30 minutes, until charred and cooked through. Transfer to a cutting board and cut into 1-inch chunks.

3. Toss the sausage with the marinated vegetables, lettuce and peperoncini. Season with salt and black pepper and serve.

beef

← pictured   80   **grilled strip steaks with green bean chimichurri**

82   california steak salad

85   skirt steak with roasted tomatillo salsa

86   flank steak with chimichurri

89   rib eye steaks with grilled radicchio

90   "steak bomb" rice and beans

↓ pictured   92   **beef, turkey and mushroom meat loaf**

grilled strip steaks with green bean chimichurri

Total **35 min;** Serves **4**

- 2 **small shallots, minced**
- ¼ **cup Champagne vinegar**
- 4 **ounces green beans, thinly sliced (1 cup)**
- 1 **cup chopped cilantro**
- ½ **cup chopped parsley**
- 1 **garlic clove, minced**
- 1 **teaspoon piment d'Espelette (see Note)**
- 1 **cup extra-virgin olive oil, plus more for brushing**

  Salt and freshly ground pepper

  Four 12-ounce New York strip steaks, fat cap left on

"When Evan brings home steaks from the restaurant, this is exactly the dish he makes," says Sarah Rich about her husband and co-chef at San Francisco's Rich Table. Adding sliced green beans to chimichurri gives the classic Argentinean herb sauce a great crunch—and ingeniously combines a condiment and vegetable side in one.

1. In a small bowl, combine the shallots with the vinegar and let stand for 15 minutes. Stir in the green beans, cilantro, parsley, garlic, piment d'Espelette and the 1 cup of olive oil; season the green bean chimichurri with salt and pepper.

2. Light a grill or preheat a grill pan. Brush the steaks with olive oil, season with salt and pepper and grill over high heat, turning once, until nicely charred outside and medium-rare within, 5 to 6 minutes per side. Transfer the steaks to a work surface and let rest for 5 minutes.

3. Slice the steaks across the grain and transfer to plates. Spoon the green bean chimichurri over the steaks and serve.

NOTE Piment d'Espelette is a sweet, mildly spicy ground pepper.

TYLER FLORENCE

california steak salad

Total **35 min**; Serves **4**

- **2** tablespoons grapeseed or vegetable oil
- **One 2-pound trimmed and tied beef tenderloin roast, at room temperature**
- **Salt and freshly ground pepper**
- **½** small red onion, finely chopped
- **¼** cup fresh lemon juice
- **¼** cup red wine vinegar
- **2** tablespoons Dijon mustard
- **¾** cup extra-virgin olive oil
- **2** tablespoons chopped tarragon
- **½** cup crumbled blue cheese (about 2 ounces)
- **½** pound green beans
- **½** pound sugar snap peas, split open
- **1** small bunch of watercress, thick stems discarded
- **4** small radishes, very thinly sliced
- **½** cup cherry tomatoes, halved
- **1** small head of iceberg lettuce, cut crosswise into 4 slabs
- **2** tablespoons snipped chives

Chef Tyler Florence of Wayfare Tavern in San Francisco tops this satisfying main-course salad with luscious roast beef tenderloin and a tarragon–blue cheese vinaigrette. He says the salad can include whatever fresh seasonal vegetables you like. He prefers crisp ones like snap peas, green beans and radishes.

1. Preheat the oven to 350°. In an ovenproof skillet just large enough to hold the roast, heat the grapeseed oil until shimmering. Season the meat with salt and pepper and cook over moderately high heat until browned all over, about 5 minutes. Transfer the skillet to the oven and roast the meat for about 25 minutes, turning it a few times, until an instant-read thermometer inserted in the center registers 125° for medium-rare. Transfer the roast to a carving board to rest for 10 minutes. Remove the string and slice the roast 1 inch thick.

2. While the meat is roasting, make the dressing and prepare the vegetables. In a medium bowl, whisk the onion with the lemon juice, vinegar and mustard. Whisk in the olive oil in a thin stream until emulsified. Stir in the tarragon and blue cheese and season the dressing with salt and pepper.

3. In a medium saucepan of salted boiling water, cook the green beans until crisp-tender, about 2 minutes. Drain and cool under running water. Pat the beans dry and transfer them to a large bowl. Add the snap peas, watercress, radishes and tomatoes and toss to mix.

4. Arrange the lettuce slabs on a large platter, scatter the vegetables over the lettuce and drizzle the dressing on top. Arrange the sliced roast beef on the salad, sprinkle with the chives and serve.

AARÓN SÁNCHEZ

skirt steak with roasted tomatillo salsa

Total **30 min**; Serves **4 to 6**

- ¾ **pound tomatillos, husked and rinsed**
- 2 **jalapeños**
- 1 **small onion, sliced ½ inch thick**
- 2 **garlic cloves**
- ¼ **cup extra-virgin olive oil, plus more for brushing**

  Salt and freshly ground pepper
- ¼ **cup chopped cilantro**
- 2 **pounds skirt steak**

Aarón Sánchez, chef at Mestizo in Leawood, Kansas, loves this blistered tomatillo salsa for its tanginess. He uses it as an alternative to red sauce on his Cheese Enchiladas with Red Chile Sauce (page 171), and on skirt steak, a flavorful cut that is ideal for weeknight dinners because it grills and broils quickly.

1. Preheat the broiler with the rack 6 inches from the heat. Spread the tomatillos, jalapeños, onion and garlic on a rimmed baking sheet and toss with 2 tablespoons of the olive oil; season with salt and pepper. Broil for about 15 minutes, stirring once, until the tomatillos and onion are softened and lightly charred in spots. Let the vegetables cool to room temperature, then scrape them into a blender. Add the cilantro and puree until smooth. Season the salsa with salt and pepper.

2. Meanwhile, light a grill or preheat a grill pan and brush with oil. Rub the steak all over with the remaining 2 tablespoons of olive oil and season with salt and pepper. Grill over moderate heat, turning once, until the meat is nicely charred, about 3 minutes per side for medium-rare. Transfer the steak to a work surface and let rest for 5 minutes. Thinly slice against the grain and serve with the tomatillo salsa.

MAKE AHEAD The salsa can be refrigerated for up to 1 week or frozen for up to 2 months.

flank steak with chimichurri

Active **15 min**; Total **40 min**

Serves **4**

Two 1-pound flank steaks

4 **cups lightly packed flat-leaf parsley leaves**

4 **garlic cloves**

½ **small shallot**

2 **tablespoons sherry vinegar**

1 **tablespoon drained capers**

Salt

¼ **cup plus 2 tablespoons olive oil**

Freshly ground pepper

"Flank steak lends itself to an assertive sauce because it has such a strong and rich flavor," says Colby Garrelts, chef at Bluestem in Kansas City, Missouri. For this chimichurri that he makes at home with his wife (and Bluestem pastry chef), Megan, Colby swaps out the usual red wine vinegar with sherry vinegar and makes the garlicky herb sauce extra-piquant with capers.

1. Preheat the oven to 375°. Remove the steaks from the refrigerator.

2. In a blender, pulse the parsley with the garlic, shallot, vinegar, capers, ½ teaspoon of salt and ¼ cup of water until coarsely chopped. Add ¼ cup of the olive oil in a steady stream and blend until thick and smooth. Transfer the chimichurri to a serving bowl.

3. Generously season the steaks with salt and pepper. Heat a very large ovenproof skillet until very hot. Heat the remaining 2 tablespoons of olive oil, add the steaks and cook over high heat until nicely browned, about 2 minutes per side. Transfer the skillet to the oven and roast the steaks for 15 minutes, until medium-rare.

4. Transfer the steaks to a cutting board and let rest for 5 minutes, then cut them across the grain ½ inch thick and serve with the chimichurri.

MAKE AHEAD The chimichurri can be refrigerated overnight. Bring to room temperature before serving.

RENEE ERICKSON

rib eye steaks with grilled radicchio

Active **20 min**; Total **50 min**
Serves **4**

Two 14-ounce boneless rib eye steaks, about 1½ inches thick

4 **tablespoons unsalted butter, softened**

1½ **teaspoons chopped thyme**

½ **teaspoon ground cumin**

½ **small garlic clove, minced**

½ **teaspoon anchovy paste**

2 **teaspoons fresh lemon juice**

Kosher salt

3 **tablespoons olive oil**

Freshly ground pepper

2 **heads of radicchio, preferably Treviso, trimmed and halved lengthwise**

The key to extra-juicy rib eye steaks, according to chef Renee Erickson of Boat Street Café in Seattle, is to baste them with butter while they sear. She also uses her delectable anchovy-cumin butter to baste roast salmon and spreads it on tartines with radish slices.

1. Let the steaks stand at room temperature for 30 minutes. Meanwhile, in a small bowl, mix the butter with the thyme, cumin, garlic, anchovy paste, 1 teaspoon of the lemon juice and ½ teaspoon of salt.

2. In a large, heavy skillet, heat 2 tablespoons of the olive oil over high heat. Generously season the steaks with salt and pepper and cook until the bottoms are nicely browned, about 4 minutes. Flip the steaks and add 2 tablespoons of the anchovy-cumin butter to the skillet. Cook, spooning the butter over the steaks, until the bottoms are nicely browned and an instant-read thermometer inserted in the center of each steak registers 125° for medium-rare meat, about 5 minutes. Transfer the steaks to a work surface and let rest for 10 minutes.

3. Meanwhile, light a grill or preheat a grill pan. Rub the radicchio with the remaining 1 tablespoon of olive oil and grill cut side down until charred, about 2 minutes. Season with salt, sprinkle with the remaining 1 teaspoon of lemon juice and transfer to plates. Thinly slice the steaks and transfer to the plates. Spoon the remaining anchovy-cumin butter on top of the meat and serve.

MAKE AHEAD The anchovy-cumin butter can be refrigerated for up to 2 days.

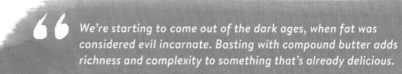

We're starting to come out of the dark ages, when fat was considered evil incarnate. Basting with compound butter adds richness and complexity to something that's already delicious.

JAMIE BISSONNETTE

"steak bomb" rice and beans

Active **30 min;** Total **50 min**

Serves **4**

- 2 **tablespoons canola oil**
- 1 **pound beef eye of round, cut into thin strips**

  Salt and freshly ground pepper
- 2 **small onions, thinly sliced**
- 6 **garlic cloves, minced**
- 2 **red bell peppers, thinly sliced**
- 1 **cup sliced button mushrooms**

  One 15-ounce can black beans, drained and rinsed
- 2 **plum tomatoes, coarsely chopped**
- 2 **tablespoons Worcestershire sauce**
- 1 **teaspoon Hungarian hot paprika**
- 1 **tablespoon mayonnaise**

  Steamed white rice, for serving
- 4 **slices of American cheese, torn**

Chef Jamie Bissonnette of Toro in Boston and New York City describes a steak bomb as a sub sandwich stuffed with a delicious mess of shaved beef, onions, peppers and cheese: "It's New England's answer to Philly cheesesteak." He upgrades this pizza parlor staple by simmering thicker strips of beef with black beans and fresh tomatoes to serve over rice.

1. In a large saucepan, heat the oil. Generously season the meat with salt and pepper and cook over high heat, stirring occasionally, until browned, 1 to 2 minutes. With a slotted spoon, transfer the meat to a plate.

2. Add the onions, garlic and a pinch each of salt and pepper to the saucepan and cook, stirring occasionally, until the onions are softened and lightly browned, about 4 minutes. Add the peppers, mushrooms and a pinch each of salt and pepper and cook, stirring occasionally, until the vegetables are softened, about 4 minutes longer.

3. Stir the meat, beans, tomatoes, Worcestershire sauce and paprika into the saucepan; if the mixture is dry, stir in ¼ cup of water. Bring to a boil, then reduce the heat to low and simmer for 10 minutes. Remove from the heat and stir in the mayonnaise.

4. Mound the rice on plates. Top with half of the meat mixture, the American cheese and the remaining meat, then serve.

I like to make big pots of stew to serve over rice, quinoa or lentils. You'd think the amount I make would last me through the week, but I tend to snack on it too much, so I give the surplus to the managers at my restaurants.

SUPER quick PREP

ROCCO DISPIRITO

beef, turkey and mushroom meat loaf

Active **10 min**; Total **45 min**

Serves **6**

- 10 ounces cremini mushrooms
- 2 cups puffed rice cereal
- 2/3 cup fat-free, low-sodium chicken broth
- 2 large egg whites, lightly beaten
- 4 garlic cloves, chopped
- 1/2 cup ketchup or low-sugar ketchup
- 1 teaspoon salt
- 1/2 teaspoon freshly ground black pepper
- 3/4 pound lean ground beef
- 3/4 pound lean ground turkey

For a healthier meat loaf, *Restaurant Divided* host and weight-loss guru Rocco DiSpirito cuts back the meat and swaps in mushrooms. He uses earthy creminis along with ground beef and turkey for a loaf that's moist and tasty.

1. Preheat the oven to 375°. Line a rimmed baking sheet with parchment paper. In a food processor, pulse the mushrooms until finely chopped and scrape into a large bowl. Add the cereal and chicken broth to the processor and pulse until the cereal is coarsely crushed. Add to the mushrooms along with the egg whites, garlic, 1/4 cup of the ketchup and the salt and pepper. Add the beef and turkey and mix well with your hands.

2. On the prepared baking sheet, shape the meat mixture into a 12-by-5-inch oval and spread the remaining 1/4 cup of ketchup on top. Bake for 30 minutes, until an instant-read thermometer inserted in the center of the loaf registers 165°. Let stand for 5 minutes before slicing.

SERVE WITH Mashed potatoes and roasted tomatoes.

MAKE AHEAD The uncooked meat loaf can be refrigerated overnight. Bring to room temperature before baking.

lamb

← **pictured**   **96**   **salt-crusted rack of lamb**

           98   grilled lamb chops with cucumber relish

         101   lamb shoulder steaks with ratatouille

         102   spiced-lamb and potato pie

         105   provençal lamb burgers

         106   lentils with butternut squash and merguez sausage

SUPER quick PREP

salt-crusted rack of lamb

Active **20 min**; Total **50 min**
Serves **4 to 6**

- **6** cups kosher salt
- **½** cup coarsely chopped tarragon
- **1¼** cups cold water
- **3** tablespoons extra-virgin olive oil, plus more for serving
- Two 1½-pound frenched racks of lamb
- Flaky sea salt, such as Maldon, for serving

For perfectly cooked racks of lamb, Mourad Lahlou of Aziza in San Francisco packs them in herbed salt. The salt crust insulates the meat, allowing it to roast evenly, and mysteriously doesn't add a salty flavor. For the best results, Lahlou positions a remote probe thermometer in the lamb before roasting.

1. Preheat the oven to 350°. In a large bowl, stir the kosher salt and tarragon into the water. The mixture should be slushy; if you squeeze a handful, it should just hold together. At either end of a large roasting pan, using half of the salt mixture, form 2 ovals slightly larger than the lamb racks.

2. In a large skillet, heat the 3 tablespoons of olive oil. Add the lamb, meaty side down, and cook over moderately high heat until

browned, about 4 minutes. Turn the racks and brown the tops and sides for 2 minutes each. Set the racks on the beds of salt and let the lamb cool slightly.

3. Pat the remaining salt mixture over and around the lamb racks to cover the meat completely. Roast for 25 minutes, until an instant-read thermometer inserted in the center of the meat registers 135°. Remove from the oven and let rest for 5 minutes.

4. Remove the salt crust and brush any remaining salt off the meat. Brush the lamb with olive oil, then cut into single chops for serving. Sprinkle with flaky sea salt.

SERVE WITH Sautéed Swiss chard.

grilled lamb chops with cucumber relish

Active **20 min;** Total **45 min;** Serves **4**

3 tablespoons extra-virgin olive oil

8 double-cut lamb chops (about 4¼ pounds)

Kosher salt and freshly ground pepper

1 English cucumber, peeled and cut into ¼-inch dice

½ teaspoon finely grated lemon zest

1 teaspoon fresh lemon juice

¼ cup golden raisins

¼ cup pine nuts, toasted

2 tablespoons mint leaves, torn

Flaky sea salt, such as Maldon, for serving

Renee Erickson of Boat Street Café in Seattle has an easy trick for extra-juicy chops: She rubs the lamb with a little oil and seasoning and lets it sit for a bit before grilling. While the chops come to room temperature, you can prepare the sweet-savory Mediterranean-inspired cucumber relish.

1. Rub 1 tablespoon of the oil all over the lamb chops and generously season with kosher salt and pepper. Let stand at room temperature for 30 minutes.

2. Meanwhile, in a medium bowl, stir the cucumber with the lemon zest, lemon juice, raisins, pine nuts, mint and 1 tablespoon of the oil. Season the relish with kosher salt and pepper.

3. Heat 2 large grill pans or cast-iron skillets over high heat. Divide the remaining 1 tablespoon of oil between the pans. Add the lamb and cook until nicely browned on both sides and an instant-read thermometer inserted in the center of a chop registers 125° for medium-rare, about 12 minutes. Transfer the chops to plates; let rest for 5 minutes.

4. Sprinkle the lamb chops with flaky sea salt, spoon the cucumber relish on top and serve.

I like to eat the lamb chops with my hands and get every last bit of meat until I've cleaned the bones.

lamb shoulder steaks with ratatouille

Active **25 min**; Total **45 min**; Serves **4**

- ¼ **cup plus 1 tablespoon extra-virgin olive oil**
- 1 **medium onion, halved and sliced ¼ inch thick**
- 1 **large garlic clove, minced**
- 1 **bay leaf**

  Kosher salt and freshly ground pepper

- 1 **eggplant, cut into ¼-inch dice**
- 1 **zucchini, cut into ¼-inch dice**

  One 14-ounce can whole peeled tomatoes with their juices, crushed by hand

- 1 **teaspoon dried oregano**

  Four 10-ounce lamb shoulder steaks, about ¾ inch thick

- 3 **tablespoons red wine vinegar**
- 6 **jarred piquillo peppers, diced**
- ¼ **cup freshly grated Parmesan cheese**

"This is a snapshot of the flavors of southern France," says Alex Guarnaschelli, chef at Butter in New York City. She sears lamb steaks to serve alongside a silky ratatouille made with two time-saving ingredients: canned tomatoes and jarred piquillo peppers. Any leftover ratatouille is terrific with eggs for breakfast.

1. In a large skillet, heat 3 tablespoons of the olive oil until shimmering. Add the onion, garlic and bay leaf, season with salt and pepper and cook over moderately high heat, stirring occasionally, until the onion is lightly browned, about 5 minutes. Add the eggplant and cook until just tender, about 3 minutes. Add the zucchini and cook until just tender, about 3 minutes. Stir in the tomatoes with their juices and the oregano and bring to a boil, then reduce the heat to moderately low and simmer until the juices thicken, 8 to 10 minutes.

2. Meanwhile, in another large skillet, heat the remaining 2 tablespoons of olive oil until shimmering. Season the lamb shoulder steaks with salt and pepper and cook over high heat, turning once, until nicely browned, 6 to 8 minutes for medium-rare. Transfer the steaks to plates. Discard the fat from the skillet.

3. Set the skillet over low heat, add the vinegar and cook, scraping up the browned bits on the bottom, until nearly evaporated, about 30 seconds. Stir in ¼ cup of the ratatouille, then return this mixture to the remaining ratatouille. Discard the bay leaf. Stir in the piquillo peppers and cheese and season with salt and pepper. Mound the ratatouille on the lamb steaks and serve.

MAKE AHEAD The ratatouille can be prepared through Step 1 and refrigerated overnight.

spiced-lamb and potato pie

Total **45 min**; Serves **4 to 6**

- ¼ cup extra-virgin olive oil
- 1 pound baking potatoes, peeled and very thinly sliced

  Salt and freshly ground pepper
- 1 pound ground lamb
- 1 small onion, chopped
- 2 garlic cloves, chopped
- 1 tablespoon chopped mint, plus mint leaves for garnish
- 1 teaspoon dried oregano
- 2 tablespoons all-purpose flour
- 1 cup chicken stock or low-sodium broth
- 1 cup frozen peas, thawed
- 5 ounces feta cheese, crumbled (1 cup)

The Chew co-host Carla Hall is a savory-pie specialist: As a contestant on *Top Chef*, she won a challenge by making the ultimate chicken potpie. For this Mediterranean revamp of a shepherd's pie, Hall adds feta and fresh mint and swaps in fried potato slices for the usual mashed potatoes.

1. Preheat the oven to 350°. In a large nonstick skillet, heat the olive oil over moderately high heat. Add the potatoes and cook, stirring occasionally, until golden brown, about 7 minutes. Drain on paper towels and season with salt and pepper.

2. Meanwhile, heat a 10-inch cast-iron skillet over moderately high heat. Add the ground lamb, season with salt and pepper and cook, stirring to break up the meat, until browned, about 5 minutes. Drain off all but 1 tablespoon of fat from the pan. Add the onion and cook, stirring frequently, until softened, about 3 minutes. Add the garlic, the chopped mint and the oregano and cook, stirring, for 1 minute. Add the flour and cook over moderate heat, stirring, for 2 minutes. Add the chicken stock, season with salt and pepper and bring to a boil. Stir in the peas and remove from the heat. Spread the meat mixture in an even layer and arrange the potatoes on top in overlapping slices. Top with the feta.

3. Bake the pie for about 15 minutes, until the cheese is lightly browned and the meat is bubbling. Let cool slightly, then garnish with mint leaves and serve.

SUPER
quick
PREP

provençal lamb burgers

Total **20 min**; Serves **4**

- **2 pounds ground lamb**
- **1 teaspoon herbes de Provence**
- **½ teaspoon paprika**
- **Salt and freshly ground pepper**
- **2 teaspoons olive oil**
- **4 brioche hamburger buns, split**
- **1 tablespoon unsalted butter**
- **2 medium shallots, finely chopped**
- **2 tablespoons white vinegar**
- **½ cup pitted Niçoise olives, coarsely chopped**
- **2 ounces Époisses cheese (¼ cup)**

Chef Jonathon Sawyer of Cleveland's Greenhouse Tavern stacks these Provençal-spiced lamb burgers with deliciously assertive ingredients, including Niçoise olives and Époisses, a soft, funky cow-milk cheese from France. If you can't find Époisses, feel free to substitute Camembert.

1. In a large bowl, lightly mix the lamb with the herbes de Provence and paprika and season with salt and pepper. Loosely form the mixture into four 5-inch patties and make a slight depression in the center of each one to help the patties retain their shape while they cook.

2. In a large cast-iron skillet, heat the olive oil. Cook the patties over moderately high heat until nicely charred outside and medium-rare within, 5 minutes per side. Transfer the burgers to a plate. Pour off all but 2 tablespoons of the fat and return the skillet to moderate heat. Toast the buns, cut side down, until golden, about 2 minutes. Transfer the buns to a plate.

3. In the same skillet, melt the butter. Add the shallots and cook over moderately high heat, stirring, until tender, about 2 minutes. Add the vinegar and olives and cook until the pan is almost dry, about 2 minutes.

4. Spread the bottom halves of the buns with the cheese, set a burger on each and top with the shallot-olive relish. Close the burgers and serve.

" I wanted a cheese that was as funky as this grass-fed lamb. So I went with Époisses, a personal favorite of mine. "

MOURAD LAHLOU

lentils with butternut squash and merguez sausage

Total **45 min**; Serves **4 to 6**

- 1 **pound merguez sausage**
- 1 **medium onion, halved**
- 8 **garlic cloves, peeled, 3 finely chopped**
- 1 **carrot, cut into chunks**
- 1 **pound French green (Le Puy) lentils (2¼ cups), picked over and rinsed**
- 3 **tablespoons extra-virgin olive oil**
- **Kosher salt**
- 1 **pound butternut squash, peeled and cut into ½-inch chunks**
- 2 **teaspoons ground cumin**
- 1 **tablespoon plus 1 teaspoon sweet paprika**
- 1 **teaspoon Marash or Aleppo pepper (see Note)**
- 1 **teaspoon harissa**
- 2 **cups vegetable stock or water**
- **One 14-ounce can crushed tomatoes**
- 1 **jalapeño, seeded and finely chopped**
- 2 **tablespoons fresh lemon juice, plus lemon wedges for serving**
- **Freshly ground pepper**

This dish from chef Mourad Lahlou of Aziza in San Francisco is a fantastic way to solve the dilemma of feeding vegetarians and carnivores at the same table: People can choose to have the Moroccan-spiced lentils and butternut squash with or without merguez sausage, which is cooked separately.

1. Preheat the oven to 375°. Place the merguez on a rimmed baking sheet and bake until cooked through, about 25 minutes.

2. In a medium saucepan, combine 1 onion half with the whole garlic cloves, the carrot and the lentils. Add enough cold water to cover the lentils by 2 inches. Bring to a boil over high heat, then cover and simmer over moderately low heat until the lentils are just tender, 25 to 30 minutes. Drain; discard the onion, carrot and garlic.

3. Meanwhile, in a large enameled cast-iron casserole or Dutch oven, heat the olive oil over moderately high heat. Finely chop the remaining onion half and add it to the casserole along with the chopped garlic and a pinch of salt. Cook, stirring frequently, until the onion is softened. Add the squash, season with salt and cook, stirring frequently, until golden. Add the cumin, paprika, Marash pepper and harissa and cook, stirring, for 1 minute. Stir in the vegetable stock and tomatoes and bring to a boil. Reduce the heat, cover and simmer until the squash is tender, about 15 minutes.

4. Stir the lentils, jalapeño and lemon juice into the casserole and season with salt and pepper. Transfer to a platter and top with the sausage. Serve with lemon wedges.

NOTE Marash and Aleppo pepper are available at Middle Eastern markets and online at *vannsspices.com*.

fish

← <u>pictured</u> 110 **pan-fried flounder with lemon butter sauce**

112 seared sole with lime sauce

115 trout amandine with creamy spinach

116 sea bass piccata with fried capers and leeks

118 crisp branzino with spinach

120 tuna steaks with plums

123 red snapper with asparagus and chorizo

125 halibut with roasted potatoes and romanesco salad

127 roast salmon with lemony basil sauce

128 quinoa-crusted salmon with spicy orange-miso sauce

JONATHAN WAXMAN

pan-fried flounder with lemon butter sauce

Total **20 min**; Serves **4**

- 2 **large egg yolks**
- ½ **cup whole milk**
- ½ **cup all-purpose flour**
- 1 **cup plain dried bread crumbs**
  Salt
  Four 5-ounce flounder or sole fillets
- 1 **stick unsalted butter, cut into tablespoons**
- ¼ **cup extra-virgin olive oil**
- 2 **tablespoons lemon or Meyer lemon juice, plus lemon wedges for serving**
  Parsley leaves, for garnish

"Flounder is an amazing fish," says Jonathan Waxman, chef at Manhattan's Barbuto. "It's firm yet delicate, flavorful and sweet." The breading he uses on the fillets is simple and versatile; it works just as well on chicken, pork, veal and other fish.

1. In a medium bowl, whisk the egg yolks with the milk. Spread the flour and bread crumbs in 2 separate wide, shallow bowls; season with salt.

2. Dredge the fish in the flour, dusting off the excess. Dip the fish in the egg mixture, then dredge in the bread crumbs. Transfer to a large plate.

3. In a 12-inch cast-iron skillet, melt 2 tablespoons of the butter in 2 tablespoons of the olive oil. Add 2 fish fillets and cook over moderate

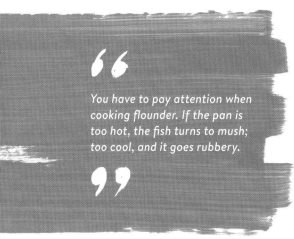

heat, turning once, until golden and crispy outside and white throughout, about 6 minutes. Transfer the fish to plates. Wipe out the skillet and repeat with another 2 tablespoons of butter and the remaining oil and fish.

4. Wipe out the skillet. Whisk in the remaining 4 tablespoons of butter and the 2 tablespoons of lemon juice; season with salt. Spoon the sauce over the fish, garnish with parsley and serve with lemon wedges.

seared sole with lime sauce

Total **15 min**; Serves **4**

- **3** tablespoons Asian fish sauce
- **1½** tablespoons palm sugar or packed light brown sugar
- **¼** cup finely chopped cilantro
- **6** fresh red Thai bird chiles, minced (seeded for less heat)
- **6** garlic cloves, minced
- **1½** tablespoons fresh lime juice
- **1** teaspoon crushed red pepper
- **Four 7-ounce skinless sole fillets, preferably grey sole**
- **Salt and freshly ground black pepper**
- **¼** cup extra-virgin olive oil

This quick Thai-inspired sauce is a weeknight miracle for any flaky white fish. Chef Kuniko Yagi of L.A.'s Hinoki & the Bird prefers making the sauce with spicy Thai bird chiles; for less fire, you can remove the seeds or substitute serranos.

1. In a small saucepan, stir the fish sauce and sugar over high heat until the sugar dissolves, about 1 minute. Remove the pan from the heat and stir in the cilantro, chiles, garlic, lime juice and crushed red pepper.

2. Heat a large skillet until hot. Season the sole with salt and black pepper. Add 2 tablespoons of the olive oil to the skillet and swirl to coat the bottom. Add 2 of the fillets and cook over high heat until lightly browned outside and just white throughout, 1 to 2 minutes per side; transfer to plates. Wipe out the skillet and repeat with the remaining olive oil and sole. Pour the lime sauce on the sole and serve.

SERVE WITH Steamed white rice and sautéed bok choy or Chinese mustard greens.

MAKE AHEAD The lime sauce can be refrigerated for up to 3 days.

ONE-POT meal

trout amandine with creamy spinach

Total **40 min**; Serves **4**

- **5** tablespoons unsalted butter
- **1** small shallot, thinly sliced
- **1** garlic clove, thinly sliced
- **2** tablespoons plain unsweetened almond milk
- **2** tablespoons heavy cream
- **1** bunch of spinach (about 10 cups)
  Salt and freshly ground pepper
- **2** tablespoons olive oil
  Four 6-ounce trout fillets with skin
- **¼** cup sliced almonds
- **2** tablespoons chopped parsley
- **2** tablespoons fresh lemon juice
- **1** small bunch of arugula, leaves torn (about 4 cups)

Evan and Sarah Rich, the husband-and-wife chef team behind Rich Table in San Francisco, rethink the New Orleans classic trout amandine to make it lighter and fresher. They keep the skin on the trout fillets and top the dish with arugula or sorrel (when in season). On the side, they serve creamed spinach simmered in almond milk.

1. In a large skillet, melt 1 tablespoon of the butter. Add the shallot and garlic and cook over moderately high heat, stirring, until softened, about 1 minute. Add the almond milk and cream and simmer until slightly thickened and reduced by half, about 4 minutes. Add the spinach and cook, stirring, until wilted, about 3 minutes; season with salt and pepper. Transfer the spinach to a bowl and keep warm.

2. Wipe out the skillet and heat 1 tablespoon of the oil. Season the trout with salt and pepper. Add 2 of the trout fillets to the skillet, skin side down, and cook over moderately high heat until the skin is crisp and golden brown, about 5 minutes. Flip the fillets and cook until the fish is just cooked throughout, about 4 minutes. Transfer to a platter and keep warm. Repeat with the remaining olive oil and trout fillets.

3. Add the remaining 4 tablespoons of butter to the skillet and cook until it just begins to brown, 3 to 4 minutes. Add the almonds and toast them, stirring, until golden brown, about 2 minutes. Stir in the parsley and lemon juice and spoon the sauce over the fish. Top with the arugula and serve at once, with the spinach.

sea bass piccata with fried capers and leeks

Total **35 min;** Serves **4**

- **6** tablespoons unsalted butter
- **¼** cup drained capers, rinsed and dried
- **¼** cup all-purpose flour
- Four 6-ounce sea bass fillets with skin
- Salt and freshly ground black pepper
- **1** medium leek, white and light green parts only, thinly sliced
- **3** tablespoons finely chopped parsley
- **1** teaspoon finely grated lemon zest
- **½** cup white verjus (see Note)
- **2** tablespoons yuzu juice or fresh lemon juice (see Note)
- **2** tablespoons olive oil
- **2** garlic cloves, thinly sliced
- Pinch of crushed red pepper
- **1** bunch of arugula (about 10 ounces), large stems removed

Andrew Zimmern, the host of Travel Channel's *Bizarre Foods*, came up with this recipe when his son, Noah, declared that a sea bass served at their local Italian restaurant was the best fish dish he had ever tasted. "My ego was destroyed, so I created this version to win him back," Zimmern says.

1. In a large skillet, melt 2 tablespoons of the butter, then cook over moderately high heat until lightly browned, about 1 minute. Add the capers and cook until the skins burst, about 2 minutes. Transfer to a paper towel–lined plate.

2. Spread the flour in a wide, shallow dish. Season the sea bass with salt and black pepper and dredge in the flour; tap off the excess.

3. Melt the remaining 4 tablespoons of butter in the skillet. Add the sea bass skin side down and cook over moderately high heat until the skin is crisp and golden, about 5 minutes. Flip the fish and cook until white throughout, about 4 minutes; transfer to plates. Add the leek, parsley and lemon zest to the skillet and cook, stirring frequently, until the leek is tender, about 2 minutes. Add the verjus and simmer until reduced by half, about 3 minutes. Stir in the yuzu juice and fried capers, then spoon the sauce over the fish; keep warm.

4. In another large skillet, heat the olive oil until shimmering. Add the garlic and crushed red pepper and cook over moderately high heat until the garlic is softened, about 1 minute. Add the arugula and cook, stirring frequently, until wilted, 1 to 2 minutes; season with salt and black pepper. Serve with the fish.

NOTE Sweet, slightly acidic verjus is the pressed, unfermented juice of unripe grapes. It is available at specialty food stores. Yuzu juice, from the Japanese citrus fruit of the same name, is available at Japanese markets and online at *marxfoods.com.*

I have been making veal and chicken piccata for decades. They're easy family standbys that I grew up eating in New York in the 1960s and '70s. I make this version with sea bass fillets.

crisp branzino with spinach

Total **25 min**; Serves **2**

- 1 stick cold unsalted butter, cut into tablespoons
- 1 large shallot, minced
- 2 tablespoons chicken stock or low-sodium broth
- 2 tablespoons fresh lemon juice
- 2 tablespoons drained capers, rinsed and coarsely chopped
- 1 tablespoon Worcestershire sauce
- 3 tablespoons minced chives
- ¼ cup plus 1 tablespoon extra-virgin olive oil
  Two 1¼-pound whole branzino, cleaned and scaled
  Salt
- 4 garlic cloves—2 chopped, 2 thinly sliced
- 1 teaspoon thyme leaves, chopped
- ½ pound baby spinach

Chef Cathal Armstrong of Restaurant Eve in Alexandria, Virginia, ate fish every Friday when he was growing up Catholic in Dublin. He has since reinterpreted dishes his parents prepared. This particular recipe is supereasy: He pan-fries whole branzino, bones and all, which helps keep the fish moist while crisping the skin.

1. In a small saucepan, cook 2 tablespoons of the butter over moderate heat until browned and nutty-smelling, about 6 minutes. Add the shallot and cook, stirring, for 1 minute. Stir in the stock, lemon juice, capers and Worcestershire. Stir in 5 tablespoons of the butter, 1 tablespoon at a time, until incorporated. Stir in the chives. Remove the sauce from the heat and keep warm.

2. In a very large skillet, heat ¼ cup of the olive oil over moderately high heat until shimmering. Season the fish with salt and cook until browned on the bottom, about 5 minutes. Flip the fish and cook, basting with the oil in the skillet, until a small knife inserted in the center of the fish near the bone feels warm to the touch and the flesh is opaque, about 3 minutes. Add the remaining 1 tablespoon of butter to the skillet along with the chopped garlic and thyme and continue basting for 30 seconds. Carefully transfer the fish to plates.

3. Wipe out the skillet and heat the remaining 1 tablespoon of oil over high heat. Add the spinach and cook, stirring, until wilted, about 30 seconds. Stir in the sliced garlic and season with salt. Spoon the spinach alongside the fish and serve with the sauce.

It's important to follow the rules for buying fresh fish: Get it with the head on and make sure the gills are red and the eyes are clear.

KATE AND MATT JENNINGS

tuna steaks with plums

Total **30 min;** Serves **4**

½ cup plus 1 tablespoon extra-virgin olive oil

½ cup dry white wine

2 tablespoons Dijon mustard

1 tablespoon coarsely chopped thyme

2 teaspoons ground fennel

   Four 8-ounce tuna steaks, about 1 inch thick

   Kosher salt and freshly ground pepper

3 plums, quartered and pitted

1 tablespoon pure maple syrup

1 tablespoon fresh lemon juice

   Freshly shaved Parmigiano-Reggiano cheese, for serving

Pairing seafood with cheese used to be a culinary taboo, but chefs like Matt and Kate Jennings of the forthcoming Townsman in Boston are debunking that rule. "My family loves meaty tuna with sweet-tart plums and the salty bite of shaved Parmesan," Matt says. "Use albacore, but if you have trouble finding it, striped bass or bluefish works beautifully."

1. In a baking dish, whisk ½ cup of the olive oil with the wine, mustard, thyme and fennel. Arrange the tuna steaks in the dish, turn to coat, cover with plastic wrap and refrigerate for 15 minutes.

2. In a large cast-iron skillet, heat the remaining 1 tablespoon of olive oil. Remove the tuna from the marinade, letting the excess drip off, then season with salt and pepper. Cook the tuna over moderately high heat, turning once, until lightly browned but still pink in the center, about 3 minutes per side. Transfer the tuna to a work surface and let rest for 5 minutes.

3. Meanwhile, add the plums to the skillet and cook over moderate heat until tender but not falling apart, about 4 minutes. Add the maple syrup and lemon juice and cook until syrupy, about 1 minute.

4. Slice the tuna and transfer to plates. Spoon the plums and sauce over the tuna, top with Parmigiano-Reggiano cheese shavings and serve.

TIM BYRES

red snapper with asparagus and chorizo

Total **30 min;** Serves **4**

- **Two 12-ounce red snapper fillets with skin, halved crosswise**
- **Kosher salt**
- ¼ **cup olive oil**
- 4 **ounces dry Spanish chorizo, thinly sliced (1 cup)**
- 2 **tablespoons minced shallots**
- 2 **pounds asparagus, trimmed and halved crosswise**
- 5 **garlic cloves, thinly sliced**
- 2 **tablespoons fresh lemon juice**
- 4 **oil-packed anchovy fillets, minced**
- ½ **teaspoon finely grated lemon zest**
- 2 **tablespoons chopped parsley**
- 1 **tablespoon unsalted butter**

Tim Byres, chef at Smoke in Dallas, has a secret ingredient for seasoning fish: thin slices of dried chorizo. "Think of them like pepperoni," he says. "The chorizo will crisp up and curl, releasing fragrant paprika oil that will flavor the fish."

1. Season the fish with salt and rub with 1 tablespoon of the olive oil. In a large skillet, heat the remaining 3 tablespoons of olive oil over moderately high heat until shimmering. Add the fish skin side down and cook until golden brown, 4 to 5 minutes. Flip the fish and cook until almost white throughout, 3 to 4 minutes longer. Transfer to a large plate; keep warm.

2. Pour off the excess fat from the skillet. Add the chorizo and cook over moderate heat, stirring, until the the slices curl. Add the shallots, asparagus and a pinch of salt and cook, stirring, until the shallots are translucent, about 2 minutes. Add ¼ cup of water and cook until the asparagus is crisp-tender and the water has evaporated, about 2 minutes. Add the garlic and cook, stirring, until golden brown. Add the lemon juice and cook, stirring, until evaporated. Stir in the anchovies, lemon zest, parsley and butter. Spoon the asparagus and chorizo onto plates, top with the fish and serve.

ONE-POT meal

CHRIS COSENTINO

halibut with roasted potatoes and romanesco salad

Total **35 min**; Serves **4**

- **1** pound baby Yukon Gold or fingerling potatoes, scrubbed and cut into ¼-inch-thick rounds
- **2** cups 1-inch Romanesco or cauliflower florets (from a 1-pound head)
- **½** cup plus 1 tablespoon extra-virgin olive oil
- **3** thyme sprigs
- **2** garlic cloves, crushed
  - Salt and freshly ground pepper
- **1** cup pitted Castelvetrano olives, halved
  - Four 6-ounce halibut fillets with skin, about 2 inches thick, patted dry
- **3** tablespoons fresh lemon juice
- **2** tablespoons Asian fish sauce
- **¼** cup flat-leaf parsley leaves

"Fish sauce brings a solid punch of flavor to a dish," says Chris Cosentino of Porcellino in San Francisco. Here he combines the umami-rich condiment with lemon juice to make a savory-tangy dressing for roasted potatoes and Romanesco—a nuttier, crunchier relative of broccoli and cauliflower. If Romanesco isn't available, you can simply substitute cauliflower.

1. Preheat the oven to 425°. On a rimmed baking sheet, toss the potatoes and Romanesco with 3 tablespoons of the olive oil, 2 thyme sprigs, 1 garlic clove and a generous pinch each of salt and pepper. Spread the vegetables in an even layer and roast for 20 minutes, until tender and browned on the bottom. Scatter the olives on top and roast until warmed, about 3 minutes longer. Discard the thyme.

2. Meanwhile, in a large skillet, heat 2 tablespoons of the olive oil. Generously season the fish with salt and pepper and add to the skillet, skin side down, along with the remaining thyme sprig and garlic clove. Cook over moderate heat until the fish is golden brown on the bottom and releases easily from the pan, about 10 minutes. Turn the fish, add 2 more tablespoons of olive oil to the skillet and cook, spooning the oil over the fish, until the fillets are white throughout, about 3 minutes. Transfer the fish to plates.

3. Transfer the roasted vegetables to a large bowl and toss with the lemon juice, fish sauce, parsley and the remaining 2 tablespoons of olive oil. Season with salt and pepper, spoon around the fish and serve.

SUPER
quick
PREP

roast salmon with lemony basil sauce

Total **20 min**; Serves **4**

Four 6-ounce skinless salmon fillets

½ **cup plus 1 tablespoon extra-virgin olive oil**

Kosher salt and freshly ground pepper

1 **cup packed basil leaves**

½ **cup packed flat-leaf parsley leaves**

2 **oil-packed anchovy fillets**

½ **teaspoon grated lemon zest**

2 **tablespoons fresh lemon juice**

1 **tablespoon drained capers**

1 **small garlic clove**

No bowls, boards or even knives are required for this recipe. While chef Renee Erickson of Boat Street Café in Seattle roasts salmon fillets, she prepares her vibrant basil sauce entirely in a blender—she even makes extra to drizzle over canned sardines for lunch the next day.

1. Preheat the oven to 400°. Set the salmon fillets on a rimmed baking sheet and rub all over with 1 tablespoon of the olive oil; season with salt and pepper. Roast for 10 minutes, until the salmon is just cooked through.

2. Meanwhile, in a blender, puree the basil with the parsley, anchovies, lemon zest and juice, capers, garlic and the remaining ½ cup of olive oil until smooth; season with salt. Serve the basil sauce with the salmon.

MAKE AHEAD The basil sauce can be refrigerated overnight.

quinoa-crusted salmon with spicy orange-miso sauce

Total 35 min; Serves 4

- 2 **tablespoons mirin**
- 2 **tablespoons sake**
- ¼ **cup ají amarillo paste (see Note)**
- 2 **tablespoons *shiro* (white) miso**
- 3 **tablespoons fresh orange juice**
- 1 **teaspoon fresh lime juice**
- **Four 6-ounce skinless center-cut salmon fillets**
- **Salt and freshly ground pepper**
- ½ **cup cooked quinoa**
- 3 **tablespoons canola oil**
- 1 **small cucumber—peeled, seeded and diced**

Chef Ricardo Zarate makes a version of this dish at Picca in Los Angeles. He coats salmon fillets with an extra-crunchy, slightly nutty crust of quinoa, a staple in his native Peru.

1. Preheat the oven to 400°. In a small saucepan, bring the mirin and sake to a boil. Whisk in the ají amarillo paste, miso and orange and lime juices and simmer gently, stirring occasionally, until thickened, about 20 minutes.

2. Meanwhile, season the salmon with salt and pepper. Press 2 tablespoons of the quinoa onto the skinned side of each fillet.

3. In a large ovenproof nonstick skillet, heat the canola oil. Add the salmon fillets, quinoa side down, and cook over high heat until the quinoa is browned, about 2 minutes. Transfer the skillet to the oven and roast the salmon until almost opaque throughout, about 4 minutes.

4. Using a spatula, carefully transfer the fillets to plates, quinoa side up. Spoon the diced cucumber alongside and serve with the orange-miso sauce.

NOTE Ají amarillo paste is a spicy Peruvian yellow chile paste. It's available in many supermarkets and online at *amazon.com*.

shellfish

132   spicy shrimp with pan-seared romaine and chickpea puree
135   green curry shrimp lettuce bowl
136   jumbo shrimp with garlic and chile butter
138   creamy shrimp, corn and tomato chowder
140   seafood, tomato and fennel stew
143   manila clams with lentils and kale
144   mussels in a saffron-citrus cream sauce
146   red coconut curry with seafood and mixed vegetables
149   peruvian seafood and rice stew
150   maryland-style crab cakes

spicy shrimp with pan-seared romaine and chickpea puree

Total **45 min;** Serves **4**

CHICKPEA PUREE

One 15-ounce can chickpeas, drained and rinsed

¼ **cup tahini**

¼ **cup *lebneh* or plain Greek yogurt**

1 **teaspoon minced garlic**

1 **teaspoon sherry vinegar**

¾ **teaspoon kosher salt**

ROMAINE AND SHRIMP

¼ **cup grapeseed or other neutral oil**

2 **tablespoons sherry vinegar**

1 **tablespoon balsamic vinegar**

2 **tablespoons minced shallot**

Kosher salt and freshly ground pepper

¼ **cup mayonnaise**

1 **tablespoon Sriracha**

1 **pound shelled and deveined large shrimp**

¼ **cup plus 1 tablespoon extra-virgin olive oil**

4 **small romaine hearts, halved lengthwise**

1 **tablespoon toasted sesame seeds**

1 **teaspoon finely grated lemon zest**

Chef Mourad Lahlou of Aziza in San Francisco performs pantry alchemy to create this elegant dish. To complement his spicy Sriracha mayo–marinated shrimp, he serves a cooling puree of canned chickpeas, tahini and *lebneh* (a thick, strained yogurt cheese, available at Middle Eastern markets). For a quick cheat, you can use store-bought hummus and mix in Greek yogurt.

1. Make the chickpea puree In a food processor, pulse the chickpeas until finely chopped. Add the tahini, *lebneh,* garlic, vinegar, salt and 2 tablespoons of water and puree until very smooth; add more water if needed for a smooth puree. Spread a scant ¼ cup on each of 4 plates. Reserve the rest of the puree for a dip or another use.

2. Prepare the romaine and shrimp In a small bowl, whisk the grapeseed oil with the sherry and balsamic vinegars and the shallot; season the vinaigrette with salt and pepper. In a medium bowl, mix the mayonnaise and Sriracha; add the shrimp and turn to coat.

3. In a large skillet, heat 1 tablespoon of the olive oil over moderately high heat. Add the romaine hearts cut side down and cook until browned, 1 to 2 minutes. Transfer to the plates, cut side up.

4. In the same skillet, heat 2 tablespoons of the olive oil. Add half of the shrimp and cook, turning once, until browned and just white throughout, 4 to 5 minutes. Transfer to 2 of the plates. Repeat with the remaining olive oil and shrimp.

5. Whisk the vinaigrette and spoon it over the romaine and shrimp. Garnish with the sesame seeds and lemon zest and serve.

MAKE AHEAD The chickpea puree can be refrigerated for up to 3 days.

EDWARD LEE

green curry shrimp lettuce bowl

Total **30 min**; Serves **4**

CURRY SAUCE

- **1** **small bunch of cilantro (3 ounces), leaves and stems, chopped (1½ cups)**
- **1** **cup unsweetened coconut milk**
- **3** **tablespoons fresh lime juice**
- **½** **small onion, chopped**
- **2** **serrano chiles, chopped**
- **2** **garlic cloves, chopped**
- **1½** **tablespoons minced fresh lemongrass, tender inner bulb only**
- **1½** **tablespoons Asian fish sauce**
- **1** **tablespoon minced peeled fresh ginger**
- **1½** **teaspoons ground coriander**
- **1½** **teaspoons ground cumin**
- **1** **teaspoon white peppercorns, coarsely crushed**
- **½** **teaspoon salt**

SHRIMP

- **2** **tablespoons unsalted butter**
- **⅔** **cup unsalted roasted cashews (3 ounces)**
- **1** **pound shelled and deveined large shrimp**
- **1** **small yellow bell pepper, chopped**
- **1** **small head of iceberg lettuce, cored and thinly sliced**
- **1½** **cups finely shredded green cabbage**

  Cilantro sprigs, for garnish

Edward Lee, chef at 610 Magnolia in Louisville, Kentucky, is an Asian-flavor investigator: He seeks out different Asian cuisines to inspire his own recipes, like this quick and fiery Thai-inspired curry served over a bowl of shredded greens. "The crisp freshness is delicious with the richness of the curry," he says. For even more crunch, Lee adds roasted cashews.

1. Make the curry sauce In a blender, combine all of the ingredients and blend at high speed until smooth.

2. Cook the shrimp In a large skillet, melt the butter. Add the cashews and toast over moderately high heat, stirring, until lightly browned, about 2 minutes. Add the shrimp and yellow pepper and cook, stirring, until the shrimp are turning pink, about 3 minutes. Add the curry sauce and simmer, stirring constantly, until the sauce is hot, 2 to 3 minutes. In a large bowl, toss the lettuce with the cabbage, then divide among 4 wide, shallow bowls. Top with the shrimp and curry sauce, garnish with cilantro sprigs and serve right away.

SUPER quick PREP

AARÓN SÁNCHEZ

jumbo shrimp with garlic and chile butter

Total **20 min;** Serves **4**

- ¼ cup olive oil
- 20 shelled and deveined jumbo shrimp (about 2 pounds)

  Salt and freshly ground pepper
- 4 garlic cloves, thinly sliced
- 2 dried árbol chile peppers, stemmed and chopped
- 1 cup clam juice or fish or shellfish stock
- 4 tablespoons unsalted butter, cut into cubes
- 1 cup cherry tomatoes, halved
- 3 tablespoons fresh lemon juice
- ¼ cup coarsely chopped cilantro
- 2 tablespoons snipped chives

"I love using shrimp when I'm pressed for time, because it cooks so quickly," says chef Aarón Sánchez of Mestizo in Leawood, Kansas. "Jumbo ones make any dish heartier and more luxurious." A spice aficionado, Sánchez briefly cooks the shrimp in a punchy Latin-style sauce made with smoky dried árbol chiles and plenty of garlic.

1. In a very large skillet, heat 3 tablespoons of the olive oil. Season the shrimp with salt and pepper, add to the skillet and cook over moderately high heat until lightly browned, 1 to 2 minutes per side. Transfer to a plate.

2. In the same skillet, heat the remaining 1 tablespoon of olive oil. Add the garlic and chiles and cook over moderately low heat, stirring, until softened, about 1 minute. Add the clam juice and bring to a boil, then simmer over moderate heat until the broth has reduced by one-fourth, about 3 minutes. Whisk in the butter a few cubes at a time until incorporated. Add the shrimp and cherry tomatoes, season with salt and pepper and simmer until the shrimp are just cooked through, about 2 minutes longer. Stir in the lemon juice, cilantro and chives and serve.

creamy shrimp, corn and tomato chowder

Active **20 min**; Total **45 min**
Serves **4 to 6**

- ½ **pound bacon, chopped**
- 1 **large onion, chopped**
- **Salt and freshly ground pepper**
- 1 **pound baby new potatoes, scrubbed and cut into ½-inch dice**
- **One 15-ounce can creamed corn**
- **One 15-ounce can corn kernels, drained**
- 1 **cup heavy cream**
- 1 **cup whole milk**
- 1 **tablespoon anise-flavored liqueur, such as Pernod (optional)**
- 2 **plum tomatoes, diced**
- 1 **teaspoon sweet paprika**
- 2 **thyme sprigs**
- 2 **parsley sprigs**
- 1 **pound shelled and deveined medium shrimp**
- 3 **tablespoons fresh lemon juice**
- 2 **tablespoons snipped chives**
- **Hot sauce, for serving**

The Chew co-host Carla Hall has a surprise ingredient in this recipe: a can of creamed corn. She uses it to add sweet corn flavor to her lightened take on chowder and to thicken the broth in place of too much cream or flour.

1. In a large enameled cast-iron casserole, cook the bacon over moderately high heat until browned, about 5 minutes. Add the onion, season with salt and pepper and cook, stirring occasionally, until golden brown, about 5 minutes. Add the potatoes and 4 cups of water and simmer over moderate heat for 15 minutes, until the potatoes are tender. Stir in the creamed corn, corn kernels, cream, milk, liqueur, tomatoes, paprika, thyme and parsley and simmer for 10 minutes.

2. Stir in the shrimp and cook until just white throughout, about 2 minutes. Remove from the heat, stir in the lemon juice and season the chowder with salt and pepper; discard the thyme and parsley sprigs. Spoon the chowder into bowls, garnish with chives and serve with hot sauce.

ONE-POT meal

COLBY AND MEGAN GARRELTS

seafood, tomato and fennel stew

Total **45 min**; Serves **4**

- 2   tablespoons olive oil
- 1   large onion, thinly sliced
- 1   small fennel bulb—halved, cored and thinly sliced
- 2   garlic cloves, crushed
-     Salt
- 1   cup white wine
- ½   pound small fingerling potatoes, thinly sliced
-     One 24-ounce can whole peeled Italian tomatoes with their juices, crushed by hand
- 1   quart clam juice
- ½   cup fresh orange juice
- 2   strips of orange zest
- ½   pound shelled and deveined large shrimp
- ½   pound skinless cod fillet, cut into 2-inch chunks
- ½   pound mussels, scrubbed
- ¼   cup chopped flat-leaf parsley
- 4   teaspoons crème fraîche

When making their otherwise classic French seafood stew, chefs Colby and Megan Garrelts of Bluestem in Kansas City, Missouri, add orange juice for an unconventional hit of brightness. "Megan and I also preserve a ton of tomatoes during the summer," Colby says, "and they're wonderful in this stew."

1. In a large enameled cast-iron casserole, heat the olive oil until shimmering. Add the onion, fennel and garlic, season with salt and cook over moderately high heat, stirring occasionally, until lightly browned, about 7 minutes. Add the wine, bring to a boil and cook, scraping up any browned bits from the bottom, until slightly reduced, about 1 minute.

2. Add the potatoes, tomatoes and their juices, clam juice, orange juice and orange zest and bring to a boil over high heat, then simmer over moderate heat for 15 minutes.

3. Add the shrimp and cod and cook until almost white throughout, about 3 minutes. Add the mussels, cover and cook until they open, about 3 minutes. Discard any unopened mussels and the orange zest. Season with salt. Ladle the stew into bowls, top with the parsley and crème fraîche and serve immediately.

SERVE WITH Crusty bread.

MAKE AHEAD The stew can be prepared through Step 2 and refrigerated for up to 4 hours. Bring to a simmer before proceeding.

RENEE ERICKSON

manila clams with lentils and kale

Total **45 min**; Serves **2 to 4**

- 1 **cup French green (Le Puy) lentils, picked over and rinsed**
- 1 **garlic clove, smashed**
- 1 **fresh or dried bay leaf**
- 3 **tablespoons unsalted butter**
- 2 **shallots, thinly sliced**
- 1 **tablespoon thyme leaves**
- 3 **pounds Manila clams or small littleneck clams, scrubbed**
- 3 **cups white wine**
- 1 **cup crème fraîche**
  Thinly sliced zest of 1 lemon
- 3 **tablespoons fresh lemon juice**
  Salt
- 1 **bunch of Tuscan kale, stems trimmed and leaves chopped**

Small, sweet Manila clams are a fixture on the menu at Renee Erickson's Seattle oyster bar, The Walrus and the Carpenter. To make a meal of them at home, she adds French green lentils and kale. The clam juices, white wine and crème fraîche create a magnificent broth that's delicious with grilled bread for dunking.

1. In a medium saucepan, combine the lentils, garlic, bay leaf and enough cold water to cover the lentils by 2 inches. Bring to a boil over high heat, then reduce the heat to moderately low, cover and simmer for 30 minutes, until the lentils are tender. Drain well; discard the garlic and bay leaf.

2. In a large saucepan, melt the butter over moderate heat. Add the shallots and thyme and cook, stirring, for 2 minutes. Stir in the clams and wine, cover and cook over high heat, shaking the pan occasionally, until the clams open, 6 to 8 minutes. As the clams open, transfer them to a bowl; discard any clams that do not open.

3. Stir the crème fraîche, lemon zest and lemon juice into the large saucepan and season with salt. Add the kale and lentils and cook, stirring, until the kale wilts, about 1 minute. Return the clams to the saucepan and stir to combine. Serve the stew in deep bowls.

SERVE WITH Grilled bread and lemon wedges.

mussels in a saffron-citrus cream sauce

Total **40 min**; Serves **4 to 6**

- 1¼ **cups Riesling**
- 4 **thyme sprigs**
- 2 **garlic cloves, smashed**
- 4 **pounds mussels, scrubbed**
- ½ **cup heavy cream**
- 1½ **teaspoons finely grated orange zest**
- 1½ **teaspoons finely grated lemon zest**
- ½ **teaspoon saffron threads**
- 2½ **tablespoons cold unsalted butter**
- **Salt and freshly ground pepper**
- **Grilled bread, for serving**

San Francisco chef Mourad Lahlou favors Mediterranean mussels, which he sources from the Pacific Northwest. "They're plump and juicy, and they don't toughen up as much as other varieties when you cook them," he says. He serves the mussels in a cream sauce perfumed with saffron and lemon and orange zests.

1. In a large, wide saucepan, combine the wine, thyme and garlic with 1¼ cups of water and bring to a boil. Add the mussels, cover and cook over moderately high heat, shaking the pan a few times, until the mussels open, about 3 minutes. Using a slotted spoon, transfer the mussels to a large bowl. Discard any mussels that do not open.

2. Pour the cooking liquid through a fine-mesh strainer into a large heatproof measuring cup. Wash the pan and pour in the cooking liquid, leaving behind any grit. Boil the cooking liquid until reduced to 1½ cups, about 10 minutes.

3. Add the cream, citrus zests and saffron and bring to a boil. Reduce the heat and simmer until slightly thickened, about 3 minutes. Stir in the butter until melted, then stir in the mussels until heated through. Season with salt and pepper and serve with grilled bread.

ONE-POT meal

red coconut curry with seafood and mixed vegetables

Total **25 min**; Serves **4**

- 1 **tablespoon extra-virgin olive oil**
- **Four 3-ounce cod fillets**
- ¾ **pound shelled and deveined large shrimp**
- **Salt and freshly ground pepper**
- 3 **tablespoons coconut palm sugar (see Note)**
- 1 **tablespoon red curry paste (see Note)**
- 4 **ounces green beans, cut into 1-inch pieces**
- 1 **small carrot, thinly sliced**
- 3 **cups low-sodium chicken broth**
- ¼ **cup unsweetened coconut milk**
- ½ **pound mussels, scrubbed**
- 1½ **teaspoons arrowroot or cornstarch**
- 1 **cup frozen peas**
- ¼ **cup coarsely chopped cilantro**
- **Lime wedges and sliced red jalapeños (optional), for serving**

Rocco DiSpirito's formula for reinventing recipes in a healthy way (without sacrificing flavor) is reversing ratios: The cookbook author and TV chef cuts back on the coconut milk in this curry and instead loads up on shrimp, mussels and cod.

1. In a large nonstick skillet, heat the oil. Season the cod and shrimp with salt and pepper and cook over moderately high heat until browned and cooked through, about 3 minutes per side. Transfer the seafood to 4 bowls and keep warm.

2. Add the sugar to the skillet and cook over moderate heat, stirring frequently, until it starts to melt, about 1 minute. Add the curry paste and cook, stirring, until fragrant and bright red, about 1 minute. Add the green beans, carrot, 2 cups of the chicken broth and the coconut milk and bring to a simmer. Add the mussels and cook over moderately high heat until they open, 1 to 2 minutes. With a slotted spoon, transfer the mussels to the bowls with the cod and shrimp. Discard any mussels that do not open.

3. In a small bowl, whisk the arrowroot with the remaining 1 cup of chicken broth, add to the skillet and bring to a simmer over moderately high heat. Add the peas and cook until heated through, about 3 minutes. Season the sauce with salt and pepper and stir in the cilantro. Pour the sauce and vegetables into the bowls and serve with lime wedges and sliced jalapeños.

NOTE Coconut palm sugar and red curry paste are available at Whole Foods Market and online at *kalustyans.com*.

RICARDO ZARATE

peruvian seafood and rice stew

Total **45 min**; Serves **4**

SALSA CRIOLLA

- **1** cup diced plum tomatoes
- **1** cup cilantro, finely chopped
- **½** cup diced red onion
- **¼** cup extra-virgin olive oil
- **¼** cup fresh lime juice
- Kosher salt and freshly ground pepper

RICE AND SEAFOOD

- **1** tablespoon canola oil
- **⅓** cup ají panca paste (see Note)
- **4** cups cooked medium-grain white rice
- Four 8-ounce bottles clam juice
- **12** mussels, scrubbed
- **8** shelled and deveined large shrimp
- **8** large sea scallops
- **4** cleaned squid, bodies cut into thin rings and tentacles halved
- **½** cup cilantro, finely chopped
- **2** scallions, finely chopped
- Kosher salt and freshly ground pepper
- Lime wedges, for serving

Chef Ricardo Zarate makes this easy Peruvian paella at Mo-Chica in Los Angeles. He starts with already-cooked rice, which means it's quicker to prepare than traditional Spanish paella. Zarate flavors the dish with spicy Peruvian chile paste (you can substitute soaked and pureed ancho chiles). For serving, he tops the seafood and rice with a bright, fresh tomato salsa called *salsa criolla.*

1. Make the salsa criolla In a medium bowl, combine all of the ingredients and season with salt and pepper.

2. Cook the rice and seafood In a large, wide saucepan, heat the canola oil. Add the ají panca paste and cook over moderately high heat, stirring, for 1 minute. Add the rice and stir for 1 minute, then stir in the clam juice and bring to a boil. Add the mussels and cook until they open, 2 to 3 minutes. Using a slotted spoon, transfer the mussels to a bowl. Discard any that do not open. Reduce the heat to moderate and continue simmering the rice, stirring constantly, until it has the texture of a very loose risotto, about 4 minutes longer.

3. Stir the shrimp and scallops into the rice and cook for 2 minutes, stirring gently. Add the squid and cook, stirring, until just white, about 1 minute. Fold in the cilantro, scallions and mussels. Season with salt and pepper and serve with lime wedges and the *salsa criolla.*

NOTE Ají panca paste, made from red Peruvian chiles, is available at specialty food shops and online at *spanishtable.com.*

MAKE AHEAD The *salsa criolla* can be refrigerated for up to 2 days.

SPIKE GJERDE

maryland-style crab cakes

Total **35 min**; Serves **4**

- 5 **tablespoons unsalted butter, melted**
- 1 **large egg**
- 3 **tablespoons mayonnaise**
- 1 **teaspoon fresh lemon juice, plus lemon wedges for serving**
- ½ **teaspoon salt**
- 1 **teaspoon freshly ground black pepper**
- ¼ **teaspoon cayenne pepper**
- 1 **pound jumbo lump crabmeat, picked over for shells**
- ½ **cup fresh bread crumbs**

These luscious crab cakes are proportionally perfect: heavy on glorious hunks of crab, light on bread crumbs. And instead of frying the cakes, Baltimore chef Spike Gjerde of Woodberry Kitchen serves them "broid" (Baltimorese for "broiled," he says). "I can't overemphasize how important it is to use fresh, carefully processed meat from blue crabs," he adds.

1. Preheat the broiler on the lowest setting and position a rack 12 inches from the heat. Rub 1 tablespoon of the butter on a small rimmed baking sheet.

2. In a large bowl, whisk the egg with the mayonnaise, lemon juice, salt, black pepper and cayenne. Gently fold in the crabmeat and ¼ cup of the bread crumbs, breaking up the crab into smaller pieces. Refrigerate for 10 minutes.

3. Pack one-fourth of the crab mixture into a ½-cup dry measuring cup and turn out onto the prepared baking sheet. With slightly damp hands, gently form it into a patty. Repeat with the remaining crab mixture; the patties will be very loose. Sprinkle the remaining ¼ cup of bread crumbs on top of the patties.

4. Broil the crab cakes for 5 minutes, or until the crumbs are golden. Drizzle the remaining 4 tablespoons of butter on top and broil for 1 minute longer. With a large spatula, carefully transfer the crab cakes to plates. Serve with lemon wedges.

MAKE AHEAD The recipe can be prepared through Step 3 and refrigerated for up to 4 hours.

vegetables

← <u>pictured</u>   **154**   **kale caesar salad**

156   quinoa salad with spring vegetables

159   sweet and savory summer fruit salad with blue cheese

160   kitchen-sink soba noodles

163   cauliflower steaks with herb salsa verde

165   roasted root vegetables with fried eggs

166   sweet potato cakes with yellow corn, basil and goat cheese

168   kale, black bean and red chile tacos with queso fresco

171   cheese enchiladas with red chile sauce

172   red kuri squash soup with ancho chile and apple

175   chickpea-vegetable stew

177   winter vegetable minestrone

178   red lentil dal with rice, yogurt and tomatoes

kale caesar salad

Total **30 min**; Serves **4**

- 1 small bunch of red or green grapes, stemmed (about 3 cups)
- ¼ cup extra-virgin olive oil
- 1 oregano sprig, plus leaves from 1 sprig
- 1 thyme sprig, plus leaves from 1 sprig
- Salt and freshly ground pepper
- Two 1-inch-thick slices of sourdough bread, torn into 1-inch pieces
- 1 bunch of kale, stems discarded and leaves torn
- ½ cup mayonnaise
- 2 ounces Parmigiano-Reggiano cheese, freshly grated (½ cup)
- ¼ cup fresh lemon juice
- 1 anchovy fillet, chopped
- 1 teaspoon Dijon mustard
- ½ small garlic clove, finely grated

Tyler Florence, chef at Wayfare Tavern in San Francisco, loves Caesar salad so much he has a special wooden bowl at home just for making it. In this version with kale, he tops the salad with herb-roasted grapes, which add pops of sweet-tart flavor. For a more substantial salad, toss in shredded meat from Florence's roast chicken (page 21) or from a store-bought rotisserie bird.

1. Preheat the oven to 400°. On a rimmed baking sheet, toss the grapes with 1 tablespoon of the olive oil and the herb sprigs and season with salt and pepper. Roast for about 10 minutes, until the grapes are slightly blistered. Transfer to a large bowl. Discard the herb sprigs.

2. On the same baking sheet, toss the bread with 1 tablespoon of the olive oil and the oregano and thyme leaves and toast for about 10 minutes, until browned and crisp. Let cool, then transfer the croutons to the bowl with the grapes along with the kale.

3. In a small bowl, whisk the mayonnaise with the cheese, lemon juice, anchovy, mustard, garlic and remaining 2 tablespoons of olive oil; season with salt and pepper. Add the dressing to the salad, toss to coat and serve.

quinoa salad with spring vegetables

Total **30 min;** Serves **4**

- 1 **tablespoon unsalted butter**
- 1 **cup red quinoa, rinsed and drained**
- ½ **cup white wine**
- 2 **tarragon sprigs**
- 2 **thyme sprigs**
- 1 **cup frozen lima beans**
- 1 **cup frozen peas**
- 3 **tablespoons fresh lemon juice**
- 2 **teaspoons Dijon mustard**
- 2 **teaspoons honey**
- 3 **tablespoons extra-virgin olive oil**
   Salt and freshly ground pepper
- 5 **radishes, very thinly sliced**

When she's cooking at home, *The Chew* co-host Carla Hall likes to prepare whole-grain salads. "They're nutritionally awesome and really filling, plus they have a great neutral flavor that's a blank canvas for anything," she says. Here, she simmers red quinoa with white wine, tarragon and thyme, then tosses it with radishes, peas and lima beans. "It's important to drain the cooked quinoa or the finished dish will be watered-down and clumpy," Hall says.

1. In a medium saucepan, melt the butter. Add the quinoa and cook over moderate heat, stirring, until toasted, about 2 minutes. Add 1½ cups of water along with the wine, tarragon and thyme and bring to a boil. Cover and simmer over low heat for 20 minutes, until the quinoa is tender; drain any excess liquid. Discard the herb sprigs. Spread the quinoa on a large rimmed baking sheet and let cool to room temperature.

2. Meanwhile, fill a large bowl with ice water. In a small saucepan of salted boiling water, cook the lima beans for 2 minutes. Add the peas and cook for 1 minute longer. Drain and immediately transfer the vegetables to the ice bath. When cool, drain again.

3. In a large bowl, whisk the lemon juice with the mustard, honey and olive oil; season with salt and pepper. Stir in the quinoa, lima beans, peas and radishes and season with salt and pepper. Serve.

MAKE AHEAD The salad can be refrigerated overnight.

sweet and savory summer fruit salad with blue cheese

Total **30 min;** Serves **4 to 6**

DRESSING

- ½ **cup plain whole-milk yogurt**
- 1 **tablespoon fresh lemon juice**
- 2 **teaspoons extra-virgin olive oil**
- 1 **tablespoon chopped dill**
  Salt and freshly ground pepper

SALAD

- 1 **pound very fresh fat asparagus, trimmed and thinly sliced on the diagonal or shaved with a vegetable peeler**
- 2 **Hass avocados, thinly sliced**
- 3 **ears of corn, kernels cut off the cobs (about 3 cups)**
- 8 **small radishes, cut into wedges**
- 1 **pound peaches or apricots, cut into wedges**
- 4 **ounces blackberries (about ¾ cup)**
- 4 **ounces blueberries (about ¾ cup)**
- 2 **tablespoons fresh lemon juice**
- 4 **ounces blue cheese, preferably Gorgonzola dolce, crumbled**
- ¼ **cup mint leaves, torn**

"Salads get a bad rap because people think, 'Ugh, it's just lettuce and dressing,'" says chef Edward Lee of 610 Magnolia in Louisville, Kentucky. "But salads can be a mix of sweet and savory ingredients, like corn and blueberries." Lee makes this salad once a week in the summer when corn and berries are at their peak.

1. Make the dressing In a small bowl, whisk the yogurt with 2 tablespoons of water and the lemon juice, olive oil and dill; season with salt and pepper.

2. Make the salad In a large bowl, combine the asparagus, avocados, corn, radishes, peaches, blackberries, blueberries and lemon juice and toss to coat. Arrange the salad on a platter and top with the blue cheese and mint. Drizzle with the yogurt dressing and serve.

SUSAN FENIGER

kitchen-sink soba noodles

Total **50 min;** Serves **4**

VINAIGRETTE AND NOODLES

- 1 **cup fresh orange juice**
- 2 **tablespoons fresh lime juice**
- 3 **tablespoons low-sodium soy sauce**
- 2 **tablespoons hot sesame oil**
- 1 **tablespoon unseasoned rice vinegar**
- 1 **teaspoon sugar**

  Salt
- 12 **ounces dried soba noodles**
- 1 **bunch of scallions, sliced**
- 2 **tablespoons black sesame seeds**
- 7 **ounces drained extra-firm tofu, cut into ½-inch dice**

VEGETABLES

- 3 **tablespoons vegetable oil**
- ½ **small onion, thinly sliced**
- ⅓ **head of broccoli, cut into florets**
- ⅓ **head of cauliflower, florets sliced**
- ½ **small fennel bulb—halved, cored and thinly sliced**
- 1 **carrot, thinly sliced**
- 1 **tablespoon finely grated peeled fresh ginger**
- 1 **tablespoon unseasoned rice vinegar**
- 1 **bunch of Swiss chard, stems removed and leaves sliced**

  Sriracha, for serving

Susan Feniger's alternative title for this noodle salad is Clean-Out-the-Refrigerator Soba with Whatever Vegetables You Have in There. Feniger, co-chef at L.A.'s Border Grill, tosses the salad in a dressing inspired by *ponzu*, a Japanese citrus-soy sauce, which she spikes with toasty, hot sesame oil.

1. Prepare the vinaigrette and noodles In a small skillet, simmer the orange juice over moderate heat until syrupy, about 15 minutes. Scrape into a medium bowl and whisk in the lime juice, soy sauce, sesame oil, vinegar and sugar; season the vinaigrette with salt.

2. Meanwhile, in a large pot of salted boiling water, cook the soba noodles until al dente, about 4 minutes. Drain and rinse under cold water; shake off any water and blot dry. Transfer the noodles to a large bowl. Add the scallions and sesame seeds and toss with three-fourths of the vinaigrette. Add the tofu to the remaining vinaigrette.

3. Cook the vegetables In a large skillet or wok, heat the vegetable oil. Add the onion and stir-fry over high heat until starting to brown, about 3 minutes. Add the broccoli, cauliflower, fennel, carrot and ginger and stir-fry until the vegetables are tender, about 5 minutes. Add the vinegar and chard leaves and cook until wilted, about 2 minutes. Add the vegetables to the bowl with the soba, top with the tofu and serve with Sriracha.

ONE-POT meal

ALEX GUARNASCHELLI

cauliflower steaks with herb salsa verde

Total **25 min**; Serves **2 to 4**

- ¼ cup chopped flat-leaf parsley
- 2 tablespoons chopped cilantro
- 2 tablespoons chopped tarragon
- 1½ tablespoons drained capers, coarsely chopped
- 6 cornichons, finely chopped
- 1 small garlic clove, minced
- 1 tablespoon Dijon mustard
- 1 tablespoon grainy mustard
- ⅓ cup extra-virgin olive oil
- 1 large head of cauliflower
   Kosher salt and freshly ground pepper
- 2 tablespoons canola oil
- ½ cup dry white wine
- ½ teaspoon finely grated lemon zest
- 4½ tablespoons fresh lemon juice
- 1 teaspoon red wine vinegar

"I can fool my family into thinking we're eating a meaty meal with this dish," says chef Alex Guarnaschelli of Butter in New York City. "And they're a tough crowd." She treats thick slices of cauliflower like beef steaks, searing and topping them with a tangy salsa verde whisked with Dijon mustard.

1. In a large bowl, whisk the parsley with the cilantro, tarragon, capers, cornichons, garlic, mustards and olive oil.

2. Cut the cauliflower from top to bottom into four ½-inch-thick steaks. Generously season them with salt and pepper. In a very large skillet, heat the canola oil until very hot. Add the cauliflower in a single layer and cook over high heat until browned, 2 to 3 minutes. Carefully flip the steaks, add the wine and cook until it is evaporated and the cauliflower is easily pierced with a knife, 3 to 5 minutes.

3. Transfer the cauliflower to a platter and sprinkle with the lemon zest. Stir the lemon juice and vinegar into the salsa verde and season with salt and pepper. Spoon the sauce on the cauliflower and serve.

MAKE AHEAD The salsa verde can be prepared through Step 1 and refrigerated overnight. Bring to room temperature before proceeding.

" I really love a good steak, but I also like a weeknight meal where I keep it in the vegetable zone. "

SUSAN FENIGER

roasted root vegetables with fried eggs

Active **15 min;** Total **40 min;** Serves **4**

- 2 **pounds mixed root vegetables (such as parsnips, celery root and rutabaga) and winter squash, peeled and cut into 1-inch dice (8 cups)**
- 6 **medium shallots, halved lengthwise**
- 2 **garlic cloves, minced**
- 12 **oregano sprigs**
  Salt and freshly ground pepper
- ¼ **cup plus 1 tablespoon extra-virgin olive oil**
- 4 **large eggs**

Although Susan Feniger isn't strictly vegetarian, much of her menu at L.A.'s Mud Hen Tavern is meat-free. At home, she tends to prepare dishes like these roasted vegetables. "It's easy when you can get so much amazing produce from the farmers' market and have it on hand," she says.

1. Preheat the oven to 450°. On a large rimmed baking sheet, toss the mixed vegetables with the shallots, garlic, oregano, 1 teaspoon of salt, ½ teaspoon of pepper and ¼ cup of the olive oil. Spread the vegetables in a single layer and roast for 25 minutes, until tender and browned; stir once halfway through roasting. Discard the oregano and spoon the vegetables onto plates.

2. In a large nonstick skillet, heat the remaining 1 tablespoon of olive oil over moderately high heat. Add the eggs and cook until the whites are crisp and set and the yolks are runny, about 2 minutes. Set the eggs on top of the roasted vegetables, season with salt and pepper and serve immediately.

ONE-POT meal

sweet potato cakes with yellow corn, basil and goat cheese

Total **30 min**; Serves **4**

- 1 **pound sweet potatoes, peeled and coarsely grated**
- 1 **medium yellow onion, coarsely grated**
- 1 **large egg**
- ½ **cup all-purpose flour**
- 2 **teaspoons thyme leaves**
  Salt and freshly ground pepper
- 3 **tablespoons extra-virgin olive oil**
- 1 **garlic clove, minced**
- 3 **ears of corn, kernels cut off the cobs (about 3 cups)**
- ¼ **cup crumbled goat cheese**
- 2 **tablespoons sliced basil**
  Lemon wedges, for serving

"A vegetarian dish can't just be a throwaway or an incomplete thought," says chef Sarah Rich of Rich Table in San Francisco. "It has to be interesting and satisfying like any other dish." She and her husband (and Rich Table co-chef), Evan, bring that philosophy home with these crisp-tender sweet potato cakes topped with charred corn and crumbled goat cheese.

1. In a medium bowl, combine the grated sweet potatoes and onion. Squeeze dry in a clean kitchen towel, then stir in the egg, flour and thyme; season with salt and pepper.

2. In a large skillet, heat 2 tablespoons of the olive oil. Spoon eight ¼-cup mounds of the sweet potato mixture into the oil and pat them into ½-inch-thick rounds. Cook over moderately high heat, turning once, until golden, about 4 minutes per side. Transfer the sweet potato cakes to a platter and keep warm.

3. Wipe out the skillet and heat the remaining 1 tablespoon of olive oil. Add the garlic and cook over moderate heat until softened but not browned, about 1 minute. Add the corn and cook, stirring, until some of the kernels are browned, about 3 minutes. Spoon the corn over the sweet potato cakes, sprinkle with the goat cheese and basil and serve with lemon wedges.

RICK BAYLESS

kale, black bean and red chile tacos with queso fresco

Active **30 min;** Total **50 min;** Serves **4**

3 tablespoons vegetable oil

8 guajillo chiles (about 2 ounces), stemmed and seeded

2 cups boiling water

3 garlic cloves, chopped

½ teaspoon dried oregano, preferably Mexican

¼ teaspoon freshly ground black pepper

   Salt

½ teaspoon sugar

1 bunch of Tuscan kale, stems discarded and leaves cut into ½-inch-wide strips (about 8 cups)

   One 15-ounce can black beans, drained and rinsed

¼ cup crumbled *queso fresco* or farmer cheese (1 ounce)

12 warm corn tortillas, for serving

According to chef Rick Bayless of Frontera Grill in Chicago, most tacos in Mexico are "warm tortillas wrapped around anything: a flavorful stew, grilled steak, scrambled eggs or salady stuff." Here, he fills tortillas with a quick stewy braise of greens and beans in a rich guajillo chile sauce.

1. In a medium saucepan, heat the oil. Add the chiles in batches and toast over moderately high heat until pliable and fragrant, about 1 minute. Using tongs, transfer the chiles to a heatproof bowl and cover with the boiling water; set a plate on top to submerge the chiles. Let stand until softened, about 20 minutes. Reserve the saucepan and oil.

2. Drain the chiles, reserving ²/₃ cup of the soaking liquid. Transfer the chiles and their soaking liquid to a blender along with the garlic, oregano and pepper and puree until smooth. Strain the chile puree through a fine sieve. Reheat the oil in the saucepan. Add the chile puree and ¾ cup of water and cook over moderate heat, stirring constantly, until slightly thickened, about 5 minutes. Season the chile sauce with salt and the sugar.

3. Add the kale and black beans to the chile sauce and cook, stirring occasionally, until the kale is wilted and the beans are hot, about 5 minutes. Transfer to a wide bowl and sprinkle with the *queso fresco*. Serve with the warm tortillas.

MAKE AHEAD The chile sauce can be prepared through Step 2 and refrigerated for up to 2 days.

AARÓN SÁNCHEZ

cheese enchiladas with red chile sauce

Active **10 min**; Total **35 min**; Serves **4**

- **2** cups store-bought red chile sauce
- **½** cup vegetable oil
- **12** corn tortillas
- **12** ounces mozzarella, shredded (3 cups)
- **4** scallions, chopped (about 1 cup)

At Mestizo, his restaurant in Leawood, Kansas, Aarón Sánchez makes an elaborate, long-simmered sauce for enchiladas. For a quick meal at home, though, he reaches for canned red chile sauce, such as one from Las Palmas. "It's old-school, very straightforward," he says. Sánchez sometimes adds shredded braised chicken to his enchiladas for a heartier meal.

1. Preheat the oven to 350°. Spread ¼ cup of the red chile sauce in a 9-by-13-inch glass baking dish. In a medium skillet, heat the oil. Add the tortillas 1 at a time and fry over moderate heat just until pliable, about 5 seconds each. Transfer to a paper towel–lined baking sheet and blot the oil.

2. In a medium bowl, toss 2 cups of the shredded cheese with the scallions and ¾ cup of the red chile sauce. Arrange the tortillas on a work surface and spoon equal portions of the cheese mixture in the center of each one. Roll the tortillas into tight cylinders and transfer them to the prepared baking dish, seam side down. Spread the remaining 1 cup of red chile sauce over the enchiladas and sprinkle with the remaining 1 cup of cheese. Bake the enchiladas until heated through and bubbling, about 20 minutes. Let cool for 5 minutes and serve.

ONE-POT meal

red kuri squash soup with ancho chile and apple

Active **20 min**; Total **50 min**; Serves **4**

- **2** tablespoons unsalted butter
- **3** pounds Red Kuri or 1½ pounds butternut squash, peeled and cut into 1-inch pieces (4 cups), seeds reserved
- **1** medium onion, sliced ¼ inch thick
- **1** ancho chile—stemmed, seeded and torn into 1-inch pieces
- **1** medium apple—peeled, cored and cut into 1-inch pieces
- **½** teaspoon cinnamon

  Salt and freshly ground pepper
- **½** teaspoon sugar (optional)

Toasted pumpkin seeds, for garnish

"Kuri squash has a unique, concentrated sweet flavor that's beautiful in soup," says Rick Bayless, chef at Frontera Grill in Chicago. (Butternut is a fine substitute.) He adds more layers of flavor with apple, cinnamon and raisiny ancho chile, and even blends in the squash seeds for nuttiness.

1. In a large soup pot, melt the butter. Add the squash seeds and onion and cook over moderately high heat, stirring frequently, until the onion is golden brown and the seeds are starting to brown, 5 to 6 minutes. Add the chile and toast until fragrant and pliable, about 1 minute. Add the squash, apple, cinnamon and 4 cups of water and bring to a boil over high heat, then simmer over low heat until the squash is very tender, about 25 minutes.

2. Working in batches, puree the soup in a blender. Season with salt, pepper and sugar, then serve, garnished with pumpkin seeds.

MAKE AHEAD The soup can be refrigerated for up to 2 days.

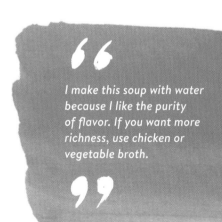

I make this soup with water because I like the purity of flavor. If you want more richness, use chicken or vegetable broth.

chickpea-vegetable stew

Total **35 min**; Serves **4**

- 2 tablespoons olive oil
- 1 cup pearl onions—blanched, peeled (or thawed frozen) and halved
- 1 red bell pepper, diced
- ½ pound fingerling potatoes, halved lengthwise
- 2 garlic cloves, minced
- 1 tablespoon finely chopped peeled fresh ginger
- 1 tablespoon harissa (North African chile paste)
- 3 cups chicken stock or low-sodium broth

  One 15-ounce can chickpeas, drained and rinsed
- ¾ cup unsweetened coconut milk
- 2 tablespoons fresh lemon juice

  Salt and freshly ground pepper
- 1 tablespoon minced cilantro

  Toasted flatbread, for serving

"Talk about Meatless Monday!" says Cathal Armstrong, chef at Restaurant Eve in Alexandria, Virginia. "This is a great vegetable dish that I cooked for the CEO of Whole Foods." He gives the stew heft with fingerling potatoes and chickpeas, creaminess with coconut milk and subtle heat with harissa.

1. In a large saucepan, heat the olive oil. Add the onions and bell pepper and cook over moderately high heat, stirring, until browned, about 5 minutes. Add the potatoes, garlic, ginger and harissa and cook, stirring, until the harissa darkens, about 2 minutes. Add the stock and chickpeas and bring to a boil. Cover and simmer over moderately low heat until the potatoes are tender, 12 to 14 minutes.

2. Add the coconut milk and bring to a simmer. Stir in the lemon juice and season with salt and pepper. Sprinkle the stew with the cilantro and serve with toasted bread.

double and
FREEZE

winter vegetable minestrone

Active **25 min**; Total **45 min**

Serves **8 to 10**

¼ cup extra-virgin olive oil

1 medium onion, quartered and very thinly sliced

1 leek, white and pale green parts only, halved lengthwise and sliced ¼ inch thick

1 carrot, sliced ¼ inch thick

1 teaspoon crushed red pepper

Kosher salt

1 large celery root, peeled and cut into ½-inch dice

1 medium rutabaga, peeled and cut into ½-inch dice

2 teaspoons sugar

1 quart vegetable broth

One 15-ounce can whole peeled tomatoes, drained and crushed by hand

One 15-ounce can cannellini beans, drained and rinsed

1 celery rib, thinly sliced

1 small garlic clove, minced

½ cup packed basil leaves, chopped

½ cup freshly grated Parmesan cheese

1 tablespoon red wine vinegar

Freshly ground pepper

"I am forever championing root vegetables," says chef Alex Guarnaschelli of Butter in New York City. "My father made so many wonderful salads from celery root and other underloved vegetables when I was growing up." Here, she simmers celery root and rutabaga in a spicy, basil-scented broth for a winter version of the Italian classic.

1. In a large soup pot, heat the olive oil until shimmering. Add the onion, leek, carrot and crushed red pepper, season with salt and cook over moderately high heat, stirring occasionally, until just tender, about 3 minutes. Stir in the celery root, rutabaga and sugar. Add the broth, tomatoes and 1 quart of water and bring to a boil, then reduce the heat to moderately low, cover and simmer until the rutabaga is tender, about 15 minutes.

2. Add the beans, celery rib and garlic and simmer for 5 minutes. Add more water if the soup is too thick. Stir in the basil, cheese and vinegar, season with salt and pepper and serve.

MAKE AHEAD The minestrone can be prepared through Step 1 and refrigerated for up to 2 days.

 *Thick slices of crusty bread and wedges of goat cheese on the side never hurt this dish, but that's just a polite suggestion.*

SUSAN FENIGER

red lentil dal with rice, yogurt and tomatoes

Total **45 min**; Serves **4**

- **3** tablespoons unsalted butter
- **1** large onion, finely chopped
- Salt
- **2** garlic cloves, minced
- **1** tablespoon finely grated peeled fresh ginger
- **1** tablespoon black mustard seeds
- **1** tablespoon ground cumin
- **1** teaspoon ground turmeric
- **½** teaspoon cayenne pepper
- **2** cups (15 ounces) red lentils (*masur dal*), rinsed and drained
- **1** tablespoon cumin seeds
- **¼** cup fresh curry leaves, chopped (optional; see Note)
- Freshly ground pepper
- Steamed basmati rice, chopped cilantro, tomatoes and serrano chile, lime wedges and Greek yogurt, for serving

In the 1980s, Susan Feniger, co-chef at Border Grill in Los Angeles, spent time cooking dal (lentils or beans) with local women at an ashram in Ahmednagar, India. She learned to make red lentils (*masur dal*) with curry leaves and mustard seeds from a particularly outspoken woman. Feniger recalls that even though the two of them couldn't communicate with words, they shared a common trait: sassiness.

1. In a large enameled cast-iron casserole, melt 1 tablespoon of the butter over moderately high heat. Add the onion, season with salt and cook, stirring occasionally, until golden, about 5 minutes. Add the garlic and ginger and stir for 30 seconds, until fragrant. Stir in the mustard seeds, ground cumin, turmeric and cayenne. Add the red lentils and stir to coat with the spices and aromatics. Add 5 cups of water and bring to a boil. Cover partially and simmer over moderately low heat, stirring occasionally, until the lentils break down to a puree, about 25 minutes. (If the lentils become dry before they're tender, add water ½ cup at a time and continue simmering.)

2. In a small skillet, melt the remaining 2 tablespoons of butter over moderate heat. Add the cumin seeds and curry leaves and stir for 30 seconds, until fragrant. Remove from the heat.

3. Season the dal with salt and pepper. Transfer to a serving bowl and top with the cumin seed butter. Serve with rice, chopped cilantro, tomatoes and chile, lime wedges and yogurt.

NOTE Fresh curry leaves are small, shiny, bright green and fragrant. They are available at South Asian markets and *kalustyans.com.*

pasta and more

182   spaghetti with veal meatballs
185   bucatini all'amatriciana with parmigiano
186   peruvian-style pasta bolognese
189   baked rigatoni with eggplant, tomatoes and ricotta
190   cauliflower and ricotta mac and cheese
192   creamy pasta with chicken and vegetables
195   rigatoni with lemony kale-and-pecorino pesto
196   rigatoni with clams, sausage and broccoli rabe
199   orecchiette with summer squash, mint and goat cheese
200   shrimp and wild mushroom risotto
203   sausage jambalaya
204   bacon and egg fried rice
207   farro and chickpea soup with chicken meatballs
209   pizza with baked meatballs
210   goat cheese and avocado toasts
213   baked polenta casserole
214   cuban frittata with bacon and potatoes

ANDREW ZIMMERN

spaghetti with veal meatballs

Active **20 min;** Total **1 hr;** Serves **4**

SAUCE

- ¼ cup olive oil
- 1 small onion, chopped
- 3 garlic cloves, halved
- 1 basil sprig
- 1 teaspoon dried oregano
- ¼ teaspoon crushed red pepper
- 1 tablespoon tomato paste
- ½ cup dry white wine

  Two 28-ounce cans whole peeled Italian tomatoes with their juices, crushed by hand

  Salt and freshly ground black pepper

MEATBALLS

- 1 pound ground veal
- 1 medium shallot, finely chopped
- 2 ounces Parmigiano-Reggiano cheese, freshly grated (⅓ cup)
- 3 tablespoons heavy cream
- 2 garlic cloves, minced
- 1 large egg yolk
- 1 tablespoon plain dried bread crumbs
- ½ teaspoon dried basil
- ½ teaspoon dried oregano

  Salt and freshly ground black pepper

- 3 tablespoons olive oil
- 1 pound spaghetti

Bizarre Foods host Andrew Zimmern has been eating a variation of this pasta for some 40 years. The tomato sauce was inspired by his mother's recipe; the tender veal meatballs are similar to the ones that legendary *New York Times* restaurant critic Craig Claiborne taught Zimmern's father to make in the early '70s.

1. Make the sauce In a large pot, heat the olive oil. Add the onion, garlic, basil, oregano and red pepper and cook over moderately high heat, stirring occasionally, until the onion is softened, about 5 minutes. Add the tomato paste and cook, stirring, until it darkens in color, about 1 minute. Add the wine and cook until slightly thickened, about 5 minutes. Add the tomatoes with their juices, season with salt and black pepper and bring to a boil. Reduce the heat to moderate, cover and simmer for 30 minutes.

2. Make the meatballs In a large bowl, mix the ground veal with the shallot, cheese, cream, garlic, egg yolk, bread crumbs, basil and oregano and season with salt and black pepper. Form into 16 meatballs.

3. In a large skillet, heat the olive oil. Add the meatballs and cook over moderately high heat, turning, until browned on all sides, about 10 minutes. Transfer the meatballs to the sauce and simmer until cooked through, about 10 minutes.

4. Meanwhile, in a large pot of salted boiling water, cook the spaghetti until al dente; drain and transfer to bowls. Spoon the sauce and meatballs over the pasta and serve.

MAKE AHEAD The sauce and meatballs can be prepared through Step 3 and refrigerated overnight. Alternatively, freeze the meatballs and sauce in resealable freezer bags for up to 1 month.

double and FREEZE

I freeze meatballs with sauce in plastic bags, then defrost them to make meatball Parmesan heros or serve over fresh pasta. You can cook a big batch and the effort for the next few meals is almost nil.

SUPER *quick* PREP

JENN LOUIS

bucatini all'amatriciana with parmigiano

Active **15 min;** Total **45 min;** Serves **4 to 6**

¼ **pound pancetta or** *guanciale,* **sliced ½ inch thick and cut into ½-inch dice**

1 **medium red onion, finely diced**

¼ **teaspoon crushed red pepper**

One 28-ounce can whole peeled Italian tomatoes, drained and crushed by hand

Salt and freshly ground black pepper

1 **pound bucatini**

Extra-virgin olive oil, for drizzling

Freshly grated Parmigiano-Reggiano cheese, for serving

Chef Jenn Louis of Lincoln Restaurant in Portland, Oregon, makes this riff on pasta all'amatriciana with just a few powerhouse ingredients. For the *salumi,* she provides options on a spectrum of porkiness, from robust *guanciale* (cured pork cheeks) to milder pancetta.

1. In a large skillet, cook the pancetta over moderate heat, stirring occasionally, until the meat is golden brown and the fat has rendered, about 12 minutes. Add the onion and cook, stirring occasionally, until softened, about 8 minutes. Stir in the red pepper and tomatoes, season with salt and black pepper and simmer over moderately low heat until the tomato sauce is slightly reduced, about 10 minutes.

2. Meanwhile, in a large pot of salted boiling water, cook the bucatini until al dente.

3. Drain the bucatini and add it to the skillet. Toss over low heat until coated in the sauce, about 2 minutes. Transfer to bowls, drizzle with olive oil and serve with grated cheese.

double and FREEZE

Total **35 min**; Serves **4**

- 7   garlic cloves, chopped
-      One 1-inch piece of fresh ginger, peeled and chopped
- 3   tablespoons red wine vinegar
- 1   tablespoon ají amarillo paste (see Note)
- ¼   teaspoon freshly ground black pepper
- 3   tablespoons soy sauce
- 1   pound dried tagliatelle
- 2   tablespoons canola oil
- ¾   pound ground beef sirloin (90 percent lean)
- 1   medium red onion, finely diced
- 2   plum tomatoes—halved, seeded and finely diced
- 1   cup chicken stock or low-sodium broth
- ½   cup freshly grated Parmesan cheese, plus shavings for garnish
- 2   tablespoons minced cilantro
-      Salt

RICARDO ZARATE

peruvian-style pasta bolognese

This pasta from Ricardo Zarate of L.A.'s Mo-Chica is based on *tallarín saltado*, a classic Bolognese-like comfort food in the chef's native Peru. Unlike the Italian version, this recipe calls for *lomo saltado* sauce—a garlicky puree of red wine vinegar, chile paste and soy sauce.

1. In a blender or mini processor, combine the garlic, ginger, vinegar, ají amarillo paste, black pepper and 1 tablespoon of the soy sauce and puree until smooth. Reserve the *lomo saltado* sauce.

2. In a large pot of salted boiling water, cook the pasta until al dente. Drain well.

3. Meanwhile, in a large skillet, heat the oil. Add the ground beef and cook over high heat, stirring to break up the meat, until browned, 3 to 4 minutes. Using a slotted spoon, transfer the meat to a bowl.

4. Add the onion to the skillet and cook over moderate heat, stirring occasionally, until softened, about 5 minutes. Add the meat and tomatoes and cook over high heat for 1 minute, then add the remaining 2 tablespoons of soy sauce and boil for 1 minute. Stir in the chicken stock and *lomo saltado* sauce and bring to a boil.

5. Add the pasta and grated Parmesan to the sauce and toss to coat. Fold in the cilantro and season with salt. Transfer to a bowl, garnish with Parmesan shavings and serve.

NOTE Ají amarillo paste, a spicy Peruvian yellow chile paste, is available in many supermarkets and online at *amazon.com*.

JONATHAN WAXMAN

baked rigatoni with eggplant, tomatoes and ricotta

Active **30 min**; Total **1 hr**; Serves **8**

- **4** tablespoons unsalted butter, plus more for greasing
- **1** pound rigatoni
- **¾** cup extra-virgin olive oil
- **2** medium eggplants (2 pounds), cut into ¾-inch dice

   Salt and freshly ground pepper
- **1** medium onion, finely chopped
- **4** garlic cloves, chopped
- **4** beefsteak tomatoes (2 pounds), cut into ½-inch dice
- **⅓** cup prepared pesto
- **1** cup fresh ricotta cheese
- **6** ounces fresh mozzarella, shredded (1½ cups)
- **½** cup freshly grated Parmigiano-Reggiano cheese

"There is no more comforting food in the world than a bubbly pasta dish straight from the oven," says chef Jonathan Waxman of Barbuto in New York City. He replaces the béchamel in this traditional baked pasta with lush eggplant. To make the recipe even healthier, he suggests using whole-wheat pasta.

1. Preheat the oven to 375°. Butter a 9-by-13-inch ovenproof baking dish. In a large pot of salted boiling water, cook the rigatoni until al dente, about 8 minutes. Drain, then transfer to a large bowl. Toss the pasta with 2 tablespoons of the olive oil.

2. Meanwhile, in a large nonstick skillet, heat ¼ cup of the olive oil. Add half of the eggplant and season with salt and pepper. Cook over moderately high heat, stirring occasionally, until golden brown, about 5 minutes. Add the eggplant to the pasta. Repeat with another ¼ cup of olive oil and the remaining eggplant.

3. Add the onion, garlic and remaining 2 tablespoons of olive oil to the skillet. Cook over moderate heat, stirring occasionally, until the onion is lightly golden, about 5 minutes. Add the tomatoes and cook, stirring occasionally, until they have broken down and thickened to a sauce consistency, 7 to 8 minutes. Stir in the 4 tablespoons of butter.

4. Add the tomato sauce to the pasta and eggplant along with the pesto and ricotta; season with salt and pepper and toss well. Transfer the rigatoni to the prepared baking dish. Top with the mozzarella and Parmigiano-Reggiano and bake for about 20 minutes, until bubbling and golden on top. Let the pasta stand for 10 minutes before serving.

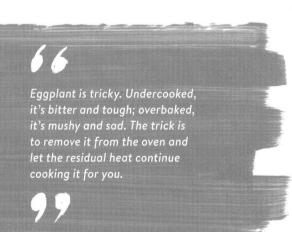

Eggplant is tricky. Undercooked, it's bitter and tough; overbaked, it's mushy and sad. The trick is to remove it from the oven and let the residual heat continue cooking it for you.

JOHN BESH

cauliflower and ricotta mac and cheese

Active **25 min**; Total **45 min**; Serves **4**

- 2 **tablespoons unsalted butter, plus more for greasing**
- 2 **cups small cauliflower florets**
- 1 **pound macaroni**
- 3 **tablespoons all-purpose flour**
- 1 **quart whole milk**
- 1 **cup fresh whole-milk ricotta cheese**
- ½ **teaspoon freshly grated nutmeg**
- 4 **ounces Gruyère cheese, shredded (1 cup)**
- **Salt and freshly ground pepper**

Whether at his New Orleans restaurant August or at home, chef John Besh is a master of rich dishes like this simple mac and cheese with cauliflower florets.

1. Preheat the oven to 375°. Grease a 3-quart baking dish with butter.

2. In a large pot of salted boiling water, cook the cauliflower florets until crisp-tender, about 3 minutes. Using a slotted spoon, transfer the cauliflower to the prepared baking dish and spread in an even layer. Add the macaroni to the boiling water and cook until al dente. Drain well.

3. Meanwhile, in a large saucepan, melt the 2 tablespoons of butter over moderate heat. Add the flour and cook, stirring, for 2 minutes. Gradually stir in the milk until smooth. Bring the sauce to a boil over moderately high heat, then reduce the heat to moderate and cook, stirring occasionally, until thickened, about 15 minutes.

4. Remove the pan from the heat and stir in the ricotta and nutmeg. Stir in the pasta, then the Gruyère, and season with salt and pepper. Spread the pasta and cheese over the cauliflower and bake for 20 minutes. Remove the baking dish from the oven and preheat the broiler. Broil 8 inches from the heat until the top browns, about 4 minutes, then serve.

creamy pasta with chicken and vegetables

Total **35 min**; Serves **4**

- 2 **cups whole milk**
- 2 **large egg yolks**
- ¼ **cup freshly grated Parmigiano-Reggiano cheese, plus more for serving**
- ½ **pound asparagus spears, cut into 2-inch lengths**
- ½ **pound spaghetti or penne**
- 2 **tablespoons extra-virgin olive oil**
- 1 **red bell pepper, cut into thin strips**
- 1 **onion, finely chopped**
- 2 **garlic cloves, chopped**
- ¼ **teaspoon crushed red pepper**
- **Two 6-ounce skinless, boneless chicken breast halves, cut into 1-inch pieces**
- **Salt and freshly ground black pepper**
- 2 **cups baby spinach**
- 1 **cup chopped basil**
- **Finely grated lemon zest, for serving**

This dish is a post-workout go-to for Cathal Armstrong, chef at Restaurant Eve in Alexandria, Virginia: He preps the ingredients in advance so that when he gets home from the gym, he can quickly make the sauce while the pasta is boiling. Armstrong likes the pasta with asparagus, spinach and bell pepper but says any vegetables will do.

1. In a medium bowl, whisk the milk with the egg yolks and ¼ cup of cheese.

2. Fill another medium bowl with ice water. In a large pot of salted boiling water, blanch the asparagus until bright green and crisp-tender, about 1 minute. Using a slotted spoon, transfer the asparagus to the ice bath to cool. Drain well. Add the pasta to the boiling water and cook just until al dente; drain.

3. Meanwhile, in a large skillet, heat the olive oil. Add the bell pepper, onion, garlic and crushed red pepper and cook over moderate heat, stirring frequently, until softened, about 6 minutes. Add the chicken, season with salt and black pepper and cook, stirring, until browned, about 3 minutes. Add the asparagus, pasta and milk mixture and bring to a simmer over moderately high heat. Simmer until the chicken is cooked through and the sauce is thickened, about 3 minutes. Stir in the spinach and basil, season with salt and black pepper and cook until wilted, about 1 minute. Divide the pasta among 4 bowls and top with lemon zest and freshly ground pepper. Pass extra cheese at the table.

It's easy to keep extra pesto in the freezer: Chill it first in an ice bath, top the container with a bit of olive oil, then freeze. Or freeze it in ice cube trays wrapped in plastic.

rigatoni with lemony kale-and-pecorino pesto

Total **30 min**; Serves **4 to 6**

- 1½ **pounds Tuscan kale, stemmed**
- 1 **pound rigatoni**
- 3 **large garlic cloves**
- ¼ **cup pine nuts, toasted**
- ⅔ **cup extra-virgin olive oil**
- 1½ **ounces Pecorino Toscano cheese, coarsely grated (½ cup), plus more for serving**
- 1 **tablespoon finely grated lemon zest (from 1 lemon)**
- **Pinch of Aleppo pepper, plus more for serving**
- **Kosher salt and freshly ground black pepper**

This is a perfect year-round pesto, particularly in the fall and winter, when basil isn't flourishing in gardens. Chef Chris Cosentino of Porcellino in San Francisco adds Pecorino Toscano, a hard sheep-milk cheese that's nuttier and milder than Pecorino Romano.

1. Bring 2 large pots of generously salted water to a boil. Fill a large bowl with ice water. Add the kale to one of the pots and cook for 1 minute, until bright green and just tender. Drain and immediately transfer to the ice bath. When cool, drain again. Transfer the kale to a work surface with some water clinging to the leaves and chop.

2. Meanwhile, add the rigatoni to the other pot of boiling water. Cook until almost al dente. Reserve ½ cup of the cooking water, then drain the pasta.

3. Transfer the kale to a blender, add the garlic and pine nuts and pulse until coarsely chopped. Add the olive oil and process until smooth. Transfer to a large bowl and stir in the ½ cup of pecorino and the lemon zest. Season the pesto to taste with the Aleppo pepper, salt and black pepper.

4. Return the pasta to the pot. Add the pesto and cook over moderate heat, stirring constantly, for 2 minutes; add some of the pasta water if it seems dry. Spoon the pasta into bowls, top with additional cheese and Aleppo pepper and serve.

TYLER FLORENCE

rigatoni with clams, sausage and broccoli rabe

Total **45 min**; Serves **6**

- ¼ **cup plus 2 tablespoons extra-virgin olive oil**
- 2 **shallots, finely chopped**
- 4 **anchovy fillets, drained**
- 4 **garlic cloves, thinly sliced**
- ¼ **teaspoon crushed red pepper**
- 2 **pounds broccoli rabe, stems separated and finely chopped**
- **Salt and freshly ground black pepper**
- 1 **pound rigatoni**
- ½ **pound sweet Italian sausage, casings removed**
- 2 **dozen littleneck clams, scrubbed**
- 1 **cup dry white wine**
- **Freshly grated Parmigiano-Reggiano cheese, for serving**

Chef Tyler Florence of Wayfare Tavern in San Francisco combines two distinct Italian favorites into a single genius dish: pasta with clams and sausage with broccoli rabe. Instead of just sautéing the rabe with the sausage, he purees it to create a quick, pleasantly bitter pasta sauce.

1. In a large skillet, heat 3 tablespoons of the olive oil. Add the shallots and cook over moderate heat until softened, about 2 minutes. Add the anchovies, half of the garlic and the crushed red pepper and cook until the anchovies have dissolved, about 1 minute. Add the broccoli rabe stems, half of the leaves and florets and 1 cup of water and cook over high heat until the stems are crisp-tender, about 3 minutes. Transfer to a blender and puree until smooth. Season with salt and black pepper. Wipe out the skillet.

2. In a large pot of salted boiling water, cook the pasta until al dente. Drain the pasta, return it to the pot and stir in 1 tablespoon of the olive oil.

3. In the large skillet, heat the remaining 2 tablespoons of olive oil. Add the sausage and cook over moderate heat, breaking up the meat with a spoon, until browned, about 6 minutes. Add the remaining garlic and cook until fragrant, about 30 seconds. Add the clams and wine, cover and cook over moderately high heat, shaking the skillet a few times, until the clams start to open, about 10 minutes. Stir in the remaining broccoli rabe leaves and florets and cook, stirring, until wilted, about 2 minutes. Discard any clams that do not open. Transfer the clam and broccoli rabe mixture to the pot with the pasta, add the broccoli rabe puree and toss to combine. Serve with cheese.

> "
> You add some of the pasta cooking water back into this dish, so don't oversalt it!
> "

JAMIE BISSONNETTE

orecchiette with summer squash, mint and goat cheese

Total **25 min**; Serves **4 to 6**

- **1 pound orecchiette**
- **6 ounces fresh goat cheese**
- **1 stick plus 2 tablespoons unsalted butter**
- **1 garlic clove, thinly sliced**
- **1 pound zucchini and yellow squash, very thinly sliced**
- **Kosher salt and freshly ground pepper**
- **1½ cups finely chopped mint leaves and stems**
- **2 tablespoons extra-virgin olive oil**

Chef Jamie Bissonnette of Boston's Coppa toils for hours making his own orecchiette but admits that high-quality store-bought brands are a fine substitute. Here he stirs pasta and thinly sliced squash with a rich sauce of fresh goat cheese and brown butter that comes together in under 10 minutes. In the colder months, you can substitute winter squash for the zucchini and yellow squash.

1. In a large pot of salted boiling water, cook the pasta until just al dente. Transfer 1½ cups of the pasta cooking water to a small bowl and stir in the goat cheese until smooth. Drain the pasta.

2. Meanwhile, in a large, deep skillet, cook the stick of butter over moderately high heat until it turns brown and smells like roasted nuts, about 5 minutes. Add the garlic and cook, stirring, until lightly browned. Add the squash, season with salt and pepper and cook, stirring occasionally, for 1 minute, until just tender.

3. Add the pasta, goat cheese sauce, mint and the remaining 2 tablespoons of butter to the skillet. Reduce the heat to moderately low and cook, stirring, for 1 minute. Season with salt and pepper and transfer to a bowl. Drizzle with the olive oil and serve.

ONE-POT meal

JOHN BESH

shrimp and wild mushroom risotto

Active **15 min**; Total **40 min**; Serves **6**

- 3 tablespoons extra-virgin olive oil
- 1 medium onion, finely chopped
  Salt
- 2 cups arborio rice
- 1 rosemary sprig
- 6 cups chicken stock
  or low-sodium broth
- 1 pound shelled and deveined
  large shrimp
  Freshly ground pepper
- ¾ pound shiitake mushrooms,
  stems removed and caps
  thinly sliced
- 2 tablespoons unsalted butter,
  diced
- ½ cup freshly grated pecorino
  cheese
- ½ teaspoon finely chopped thyme

"Risotto without the work" sounds like a dubious promise, but John Besh swears it's possible: Instead of adding a little stock at a time and stirring constantly, Besh, the chef at August in New Orleans, adds the stock only a few times and stirs just occasionally. It's an unconventional method that still yields silky results.

1. In a large, heavy saucepan, heat the olive oil until shimmering. Add the onion, season with salt and cook over high heat, stirring frequently, until softened, 4 to 5 minutes. Add the rice and cook, stirring, for 1 minute. Add the rosemary and 2 cups of the stock and bring to a boil. Cover, reduce the heat to moderately low and simmer for 5 minutes. Stir in another 2 cups of the stock and bring to a boil over high heat. Cover, reduce the heat to moderately low and simmer for 10 minutes.

2. Season the shrimp with salt and pepper. Stir into the rice along with the mushrooms and the remaining 2 cups of stock and cook over moderate heat, stirring occasionally, until the shrimp are just cooked and the rice is tender, about 10 minutes. Discard the rosemary. Stir in the butter and cheese and season with salt and pepper. Sprinkle the thyme on top and serve immediately.

sausage jambalaya

Active **20 min**; Total **45 min**

Serves **4 to 6**

- 1 tablespoon canola oil
- ¾ pound andouille sausage, sliced ¼ inch thick
- ¼ pound breakfast sausage, casings removed
- 1 large onion, diced
- ½ green bell pepper, diced
- 1 celery rib, diced
- 1 garlic clove, chopped
- 2 cups white rice
- 1 bay leaf
- ½ teaspoon dried thyme
- Salt and freshly ground pepper
- 1 quart chicken stock or canned low-sodium broth
- One 14½-ounce can chopped tomatoes
- 3 scallions, chopped
- Tabasco or other hot sauce, for serving

Chef John Besh of August in New Orleans says he's been eating jambalaya ever since he could chew. For this quick, simplified version of the Creole classic, he insists on high-quality, well-seasoned meat because the andouille and breakfast sausage provide the bulk of the flavor in the dish.

1. Heat a large enameled cast-iron casserole until hot. Add the oil and both sausages and cook over moderate heat, stirring to break up the breakfast sausage, until the fat renders and the sausages brown, about 8 minutes.

2. Add the onion and cook, stirring frequently, until softened, about 5 minutes. Add the bell pepper, celery and garlic and cook, stirring occasionally, until the bell pepper and celery are crisp-tender, about 5 minutes. Stir in the rice, bay leaf and thyme, season with salt and pepper and cook, stirring, for 3 minutes.

3. Add the stock and tomatoes and bring to a boil over high heat. Reduce the heat to moderately low, cover and simmer until the rice is tender, about 20 minutes. Fold in the scallions and serve with Tabasco.

ONE-POT meal

SPIKE GJERDE

bacon and egg fried rice

Total **35 min**; Serves **4**

- **2** tablespoons canola oil
- **6** strips of bacon, chopped (¾ cup)
- **4** cups chopped mixed vegetables, such as onions, broccoli, carrots, bell peppers and snap peas

  Salt and freshly ground pepper

  One 1-inch piece of fresh ginger, peeled and julienned (1 tablespoon)
- **3** garlic cloves, very thinly sliced
- **6** cups cooked white rice
- **1** tablespoon tamari or soy sauce
- **4** large eggs

  Hot sauce, for serving

Chef Spike Gjerde of Woodberry Kitchen in Baltimore has devised a great weeknight clean-out-your-fridge dinner, cooking with whatever vegetables he has on hand. Gjerde makes the meal completely gluten-free for his wife, who has celiac disease: He adds a splash of wheat-free tamari instead of soy sauce.

1. Preheat the oven to 400°. In a large nonstick ovenproof skillet or wok, heat 1 tablespoon of the oil over moderately high heat. Add the bacon and cook, stirring, until browned and crisp, about 6 minutes. With a slotted spoon, transfer to paper towels to drain.

2. Add the remaining 1 tablespoon of oil to the skillet. Add the vegetables, season with salt and pepper and stir-fry over moderately high heat until crisp-tender, 3 to 5 minutes. Add the ginger and garlic and stir-fry for 2 minutes. Add the rice and stir-fry until heated through, about 2 minutes. Stir in the bacon and tamari and season with salt and pepper.

3. Using the back of a spoon, make 4 nests in the rice. Crack an egg into each nest. Transfer the skillet to the oven and bake for 5 minutes, until the egg whites are just set and the yolks are runny. Serve the fried rice at once, with hot sauce.

JENN LOUIS

farro and chickpea soup with chicken meatballs

Active **20 min**; Total **50 min**; Serves **4**

MEATBALLS

- 1 **pound ground dark-meat chicken**
- 1 **large egg, beaten**
- 4 **garlic cloves, minced**
- 2 **tablespoons freshly grated Parmigiano-Reggiano cheese**
- 1½ **teaspoons kosher salt**
- 1 **teaspoon chopped sage**
- ½ **teaspoon freshly ground pepper**

SOUP

- 2 **tablespoons extra-virgin olive oil, plus more for drizzling**
- 1 **small onion, finely diced**
- 2 **medium carrots, finely diced**
- 4 **sage leaves**
  - **Kosher salt and freshly ground pepper**
  - **One 15-ounce can chickpeas**
- 1 **cup cooked farro**
- 2 **quarts chicken stock or low-sodium broth**
- 4 **loosely packed cups chopped tender mustard greens**
  - **Freshly grated Parmigiano-Reggiano cheese, for serving**

For this soothing soup, chef Jenn Louis of Lincoln Restaurant in Portland, Oregon, makes her meatballs extra-large (about the size of golf balls) for two reasons: They are quicker to prepare and remain more tender.

1. Make the meatballs Combine all of the ingredients in a large bowl. Cover and refrigerate for 30 minutes.

2. Meanwhile, make the soup In a large soup pot, heat the 2 tablespoons of olive oil. Add the onion, carrots, sage and a pinch each of salt and pepper. Cook over moderately high heat, stirring occasionally, until the onion is translucent, about 5 minutes. Add the chickpeas, farro and chicken stock and bring to a boil, then reduce the heat to maintain a steady simmer.

3. Gently form the chicken mixture into 12 meatballs, then lower them into the soup and simmer until just cooked through, about 12 minutes. Stir in the mustard greens and cook until just wilted, about 30 seconds. Season the soup with salt and pepper and ladle into bowls. Top with cheese, drizzle with olive oil and serve.

MAKE AHEAD The meatball mixture can be refrigerated overnight.

double and FREEZE

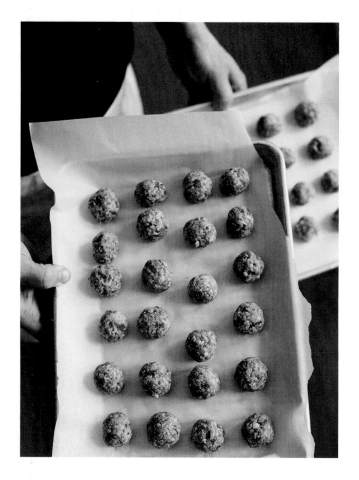

double and FREEZE

KATE AND MATT JENNINGS

pizza with baked meatballs

Total **45 min**; Serves **4**

- 1 tablespoon olive oil, plus more for brushing
- 1 large egg
- 2 tablespoons panko
- 2 garlic cloves, minced
- ¼ cup finely chopped flat-leaf parsley
- 1 cup freshly grated Parmigiano-Reggiano cheese

    Kosher salt and freshly ground pepper

- 1 pound ground beef chuck

    One 28-ounce can crushed tomatoes

    Two 8-ounce balls of pizza dough, at room temperature

- 1 cup basil leaves

When he lived in Florence, Matt Jennings often made this pizza with leftover vegetables, cheese and olives. Now he bakes it at home with Kate, his wife and co-chef at the forthcoming Townsman in Boston. They top their pizza with meatballs and sauce left over from a pasta dinner.

1. Preheat the oven to 450°. Brush a large ceramic baking dish with olive oil or line 2 baking sheets with parchment paper. In a large bowl, whisk the egg. Stir in the panko, garlic, parsley, ¼ cup of the cheese, 1 teaspoon of salt and ½ teaspoon of pepper. Add the ground beef and gently knead to combine. Form the mixture into 1-inch meatballs and transfer to the baking dish. Bake for about 10 minutes, turning once, until browned.

2. Meanwhile, in a large saucepan, heat the 1 tablespoon of olive oil. Add the crushed tomatoes and cook over moderately high heat until bubbling.

3. Add the meatballs to the tomato sauce, cover partially and simmer over moderately low heat until the meatballs are cooked through, about 10 minutes. With a large spoon, mash the meatballs into large chunks. Remove from the heat.

4. Meanwhile, brush 2 large baking sheets with olive oil and preheat in the upper and lower thirds of the oven. On a lightly floured work surface, cut each ball of dough in half. Roll each piece into a 10-inch oval. Arrange the dough on the heated baking sheets and bake for about 7 minutes, shifting the pans halfway through, until lightly golden on top and browned on the bottom.

5. Spread the meatball sauce over the crusts, leaving a ½-inch border. Sprinkle with the remaining ¾ cup of cheese. Bake for about 5 minutes, until the crust is crisp on the bottom and the cheese is melted. Scatter basil leaves over the pizzas and serve hot.

SUSAN FENIGER

goat cheese and avocado toasts

Total **10 min**; Serves **4**

- 2 Hass avocados—halved, pitted and peeled
- 2 ounces mild soft goat cheese (¼ cup)
- 1 tablespoon fresh lemon juice
- 4 dashes of Tabasco
- ⅛ teaspoon freshly ground pepper
  Kosher salt
- 8 slices of pumpernickel bread, toasted
- 2 tomatoes, thinly sliced
  Extra-virgin olive oil, for drizzling
  Sea salt, for serving

"I make these toasts, grab some potato chips—my secret love—and fix a yummy drink," says Susan Feniger, co-chef at Border Grill in Los Angeles. "That's a late-night dinner!" To change it up, she sometimes broils the avocado toasts for a couple of minutes before topping them with tomatoes, or she'll spread the avocado on rice crackers instead of bread.

In a medium bowl, mash the avocados with the goat cheese, lemon juice, Tabasco and pepper until the mixture is still a bit lumpy. Season with kosher salt. Spread the avocado mixture on the pumpernickel toasts and top with tomatoes. Drizzle with olive oil, sprinkle with sea salt and serve.

SUPER quick PREP

SUPER
quick
PREP

baked polenta casserole

Active **10 min**; Total **35 min**
Serves **8**

- **4 cups whole milk**
- **2 cups instant polenta**
- **2 cups freshly grated Pecorino Romano cheese**
- **4 tablespoons unsalted butter**
  Pinch of freshly grated nutmeg
  Salt and freshly ground pepper
- **2 large eggs, lightly beaten**
- **2 cups tomato sauce**

Chef Jonathon Sawyer of Cleveland's Greenhouse Tavern says this was the first meal that his wife, Amelia, ever cooked for him. It's her take on Roman-style gnocchi—fluffy polenta and Pecorino Romano baked under a blanket of tangy tomato sauce—which is much quicker to make than the more familiar dumpling-style gnocchi.

Preheat the oven to 350°. In a large saucepan, combine the milk with 3 cups of water and bring to a boil. Slowly whisk in the polenta. Cook over low heat, whisking constantly, until the polenta is thick, about 3 minutes. Whisk in 1½ cups of the cheese, the butter and the nutmeg and season with salt and pepper. Whisk in the eggs in a slow, steady stream and transfer the polenta mixture to a 9-by-13-inch baking dish. Spread the tomato sauce over the polenta and sprinkle with the remaining ½ cup of cheese. Bake until the cheese is melted and the tomato sauce is bubbling, about 20 minutes. Let the baked polenta rest for 5 minutes before serving.

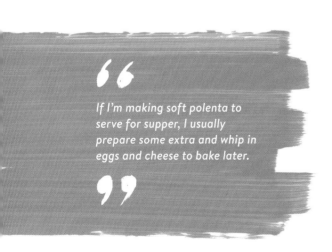

If I'm making soft polenta to serve for supper, I usually prepare some extra and whip in eggs and cheese to bake later.

ONE-POT meal

cuban frittata with bacon and potatoes

Total **45 min;** Serves **4**

- **¼** pound slab bacon, cut into ½-inch dice (about ½ cup)
- **⅓** cup olive oil
- **1** medium Yukon Gold potato, scrubbed and cut into ½-inch dice (about 1 cup)
- **1** medium sweet onion, cut into ½-inch dice (about 2 cups)
- **6** large eggs beaten with ½ teaspoon kosher salt
- **1** large bunch of watercress, thick stems discarded and the rest coarsely chopped
- **1 to 2 tablespoons apple cider vinegar**
- **Kosher salt and freshly ground pepper**

This rich, custardy frittata from chef Tim Byres of Smoke in Dallas is an inspired way to have breakfast for dinner. Based on the Cuban *tortilla de papas* that his Cuban mother-in-law makes, it's studded with potatoes, onion and slab bacon, then topped with a peppery watercress salad.

1. In a 10-inch nonstick skillet, cook the bacon in the olive oil over moderate heat, stirring occasionally, until golden brown, about 10 minutes. With a slotted spoon, transfer the bacon to a medium bowl.

2. Add the potatoes to the skillet in a single layer and cook over high heat until browned on the bottom. Reduce the heat to moderately high and cook, stirring occasionally, until tender, about 12 minutes. With a slotted spoon, add the potatoes to the bowl with the bacon.

3. Add the onion to the skillet and cook over moderate heat, stirring occasionally, until softened, about 5 minutes. Reduce the heat to low and stir in the bacon and potatoes. Spread in an even layer, then pour in the beaten eggs. Cook, without stirring, until the eggs are just set, about 6 minutes; they will be a little moist on top.

4. Run a rubber spatula around the edge of the eggs. Invert a 12-inch plate over the pan. Wearing oven mitts, quickly and carefully invert the skillet and plate to release the eggs. Slide the eggs back into the skillet and cook over low heat until set, about 4 minutes. Carefully slide the tortilla onto a serving plate.

5. In a large bowl, toss the watercress with 1 tablespoon of the vinegar and season with salt and pepper; add more vinegar to taste. Cut the tortilla into wedges, top with the watercress salad and serve.

desserts

218 fruit and nut crumb bars

221 roasted peach cobbler with vanilla ice cream and balsamic syrup

223 rhubarb pudding cake

224 brown sugar crumb cake

↓ **pictured** **226** **mexican chocolate chip–pumpkin seed cake**

229 oatmeal-cherry cookies

230 rosemary-cornmeal sugar cookies

232 dark chocolate pudding

235 popcorn pudding

KATE AND MATT JENNINGS

fruit and nut crumb bars

Active **15 min**; Total **1 hr plus cooling**

Makes **one dozen bars**

- 2 **sticks unsalted butter, softened, plus more for greasing**
- 2 **cups all-purpose flour**
- 2 **cups old-fashioned rolled oats**
- 1¼ **cups packed light brown sugar**
- ½ **teaspoon baking soda**
- ½ **teaspoon salt**
- 2 **Granny Smith apples—peeled, cored and sliced ¼ inch thick**
- 2 **tablespoons fresh lemon juice**
- 2 **tablespoons granulated sugar**
- ¼ **teaspoon cinnamon**
- ¼ **cup sliced almonds**

Chefs Kate and Matt Jennings of the forthcoming Townsman in Boston often make everything from scratch, including the preserves they like to layer in these simple bars. Alternatively, you can use your favorite jarred jam or fresh fruit (apples or pears in the fall and winter, berries or stone fruits in the warmer months).

1. Preheat the oven to 350°. Butter a 9-by-13-inch metal baking pan. In a large bowl, combine the flour with the oats, brown sugar, baking soda and salt. Add the 2 sticks of butter and, with your fingers, rub it into the mixture evenly. Pat all but 1 cup of the crumble into the baking pan in an even layer and bake until the top is golden, about 15 minutes.

2. Meanwhile, in a large bowl, toss the apples with the lemon juice, granulated sugar and cinnamon. Spread the apples evenly over the dough in the pan, then sprinkle with the almonds and the remaining crumble. Bake for about 35 minutes, until the apples are tender and the juices are bubbling. Let cool before slicing and serving.

MAKE AHEAD The bars can be stored in an airtight container for up to 2 days.

My mother would make a simple version of this dessert every August, when peaches were at their peak. Their juiciness makes them the perfect fruit for a cobbler.

ANDREW ZIMMERN

roasted peach cobbler with vanilla ice cream and balsamic syrup

Active **15 min;** Total **50 min**
Serves **6**

- 8 large ripe peaches (4 pounds), peeled and cut into ½-inch-thick wedges
- 3 tablespoons packed light brown sugar
- ½ cup all-purpose flour
- ¼ cup granulated sugar
- ¼ teaspoon baking soda
- ¼ teaspoon kosher salt
- 4 tablespoons cold unsalted butter, diced
- 1 large egg yolk
- ¼ teaspoon pure vanilla extract
- 1 tablespoon fresh lemon juice
- 1 pint vanilla ice cream, for serving
- 1 tablespoon balsamic vinegar syrup

"I'm no pastry chef, but I bake a killer cobbler," says Andrew Zimmern, host of *Bizarre Foods*. He tops the dessert with vanilla ice cream and thick, rich aged balsamic syrup. Two favorites: Malpighi Saporoso *condimento balsamico* and Noble Tonic 05: XO, which is aged in bourbon casks.

1. Preheat the broiler on high and position a rack about 6 inches from the heat. In a large bowl, toss the peaches with the brown sugar and scrape them onto a rimmed baking sheet. Broil the peaches for about 15 minutes, flipping them halfway through, until caramelized and juicy. Let the peaches cool slightly. Lower the oven temperature to 375°.

2. Meanwhile, in another large bowl, combine the flour, granulated sugar, baking soda and salt. Add the butter and, with your fingers, rub it into the mixture evenly. Stir in the egg yolk and vanilla. Refrigerate the crumb topping.

3. In a medium bowl, toss the cooled peaches with the lemon juice; divide among six 8-ounce ramekins. Sprinkle with the crumb topping, transfer the ramekins to a baking sheet and bake until the topping is golden and the fruit is bubbling, about 20 minutes. Let cool for 5 minutes, then serve with the vanilla ice cream and a drizzle of the balsamic syrup.

rhubarb pudding cake

Active **15 min**; Total **45 min plus cooling**

Makes **one 9-inch cake**

- **6** tablespoons unsalted butter, at room temperature, plus more for greasing
- **1** cup all-purpose flour
- **1** teaspoon baking powder
- **1** teaspoon cinnamon
- **¼** teaspoon salt
- **½** cup packed light brown sugar
- **1** cup granulated sugar
- **1** teaspoon pure vanilla extract
- **1** large egg
- **½** cup whole milk
- **¾** pound rhubarb stalks, cut into ½-inch slices (about 3½ cups)

When *The Chew* co-host Carla Hall wants to lighten a dessert, she adds fruit. In this supermoist, cinnamony pudding cake, she uses rhubarb (technically a vegetable but treated like fruit here). However, Hall says you can also add strawberries, or swap in peaches or berries.

1. Preheat the oven to 350°. Butter a 9-inch-square glass or ceramic baking dish.

2. In a medium bowl, whisk the flour with the baking powder, cinnamon and salt. In a large bowl, using an electric mixer, beat the 6 tablespoons of butter with the brown sugar and ½ cup of the granulated sugar at medium-high speed until pale and fluffy, about 5 minutes. Reduce the speed to medium and beat in the vanilla and egg. Scrape down the side and bottom of the bowl. At low speed, beat in the dry ingredients and milk in 3 alternating additions, scraping down the bowl as necessary.

3. In another medium bowl, toss the rhubarb with the remaining ½ cup of granulated sugar. Spread in the bottom of the prepared baking dish. Dollop the cake batter over the rhubarb and spread it evenly. Bake for 30 minutes, until the cake is golden brown and a cake tester inserted in the center comes out clean. Let the cake cool in the pan on a wire rack and serve warm or at room temperature.

SERVE WITH Whipped cream.

MAKE AHEAD The cake can be kept at room temperature for up to 6 hours.

brown sugar crumb cake

Active **20 min**; Total **50 min plus cooling**
Makes **one 9-inch cake**

CRUMBS

- ¼ cup plus 2 tablespoons packed light brown sugar
- 2 tablespoons all-purpose flour
- ⅛ teaspoon cinnamon
- Pinch of kosher salt
- 2 tablespoons cold unsalted butter, diced
- 2 tablespoons old-fashioned rolled oats
- 2 tablespoons chopped pecans (optional)

CAKE

- 1½ cups all-purpose flour
- 1 teaspoon baking powder
- ½ teaspoon baking soda
- ½ teaspoon cinnamon
- ¼ teaspoon freshly grated nutmeg
- 1 stick unsalted butter, at room temperature
- 1½ cups packed light brown sugar
- ¾ teaspoon kosher salt
- 1 cup sour cream, at room temperature
- 2 large eggs, at room temperature
- ½ teaspoon pure vanilla extract

"Everyone likes something warm out of the oven," says Megan Garrelts, pastry chef at Bluestem in Kansas City, Missouri. Megan and her husband (and Bluestem chef), Colby, serve this moist, not-too-sweet cake warm along with lemon sherbet. They toast any leftover cake and top it with butter and jam for breakfast.

1. Preheat the oven to 350°. Coat a 9-inch-square cake pan with vegetable oil spray.

2. Make the crumbs In a food processor, pulse the brown sugar with the flour, cinnamon and salt. Add the butter and pulse until the mixture has a sandy texture. Add the oats and pecans and pulse until incorporated. Transfer the crumbs to a bowl and freeze until ready to use.

3. Make the cake In a medium bowl, combine the flour with the baking powder, baking soda, cinnamon and nutmeg. Sift the mixture onto a sheet of parchment paper.

4. In a large bowl, using an electric mixer, cream the butter with the brown sugar and salt at medium-high speed until fluffy, about 5 minutes; scrape the bowl. Add the sour cream and beat until smooth, about 2 minutes. Beat in the eggs one at a time at medium speed, scraping the bowl after each addition. Beat in the vanilla. At low speed, beat in the flour mixture in 3 additions, scraping the bowl as needed.

5. Spread the batter in the prepared pan and scatter the frozen crumbs on top. Bake for 30 minutes, until golden brown and a toothpick inserted in the center comes out clean. Transfer to a wire rack and let cool. Cut into 12 squares and serve warm or at room temperature.

MAKE AHEAD The crumbs can be frozen in an airtight container for up to 1 week. The cake can be kept at room temperature for up to 3 days.

SUPER quick PREP

mexican chocolate chip–pumpkin seed cake

Active **10 min**; Total **1 hr 10 min**

Makes **one 9-inch cake**

- 1   stick unsalted butter, cut into ½-inch dice and softened, plus more for greasing
- 1¾ cups salted toasted pumpkin seeds
- 1   cup plus 2 tablespoons granulated sugar
- 3   large eggs, at room temperature
- 1   tablespoon tequila
- ⅓   cup all-purpose flour
- ¼   teaspoon baking powder
- 3   ounces Mexican chocolate, finely chopped (about ¾ cup)
- 2   teaspoons confectioners' sugar

Every time Rick Bayless travels to Mexico, he buys *pepitorias*—a kind of pumpkin seed–packed brittle—immediately after he lands. Bayless, chef at Topolobampo in Chicago, incorporates the flavor of that street food here in a fluffy cake and adds Mexican chocolate, which is spiced with cinnamon and vanilla.

1. Preheat the oven to 350°. Butter a 9-inch cake pan and line the bottom with parchment paper. Butter the paper. Sprinkle ½ cup of the pumpkin seeds in the pan and dust with 2 tablespoons of the granulated sugar.

2. In a food processor, pulse the remaining 1¼ cups of pumpkin seeds and 1 cup of granulated sugar until the mixture resembles wet sand. Add the eggs, tequila and 1 stick of butter and pulse until smooth. Add the flour and baking powder and pulse just until incorporated. Add the chocolate and pulse until mixed, about 4 pulses.

3. Scrape the batter into the prepared pan and bake in the lower third of the oven for about 50 minutes, until a toothpick inserted in the center of the cake comes out clean; rotate the pan halfway through baking. Let the cake cool in the pan for 10 minutes.

4. Invert the cake onto a plate and peel off the parchment paper. Dust the cake with the confectioners' sugar and serve warm or at room temperature.

MAKE AHEAD The cake can be kept in an airtight container at room temperature for up to 1 day.

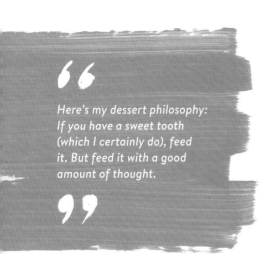

Here's my dessert philosophy: If you have a sweet tooth (which I certainly do), feed it. But feed it with a good amount of thought.

oatmeal-cherry cookies

Active **30 min**; Total **1 hr plus cooling**

Makes **18 cookies**

- ¾ cup all-purpose flour
- ½ cup whole-wheat flour
- ½ teaspoon baking soda
- ½ teaspoon kosher salt
- ½ teaspoon cinnamon
- ¼ teaspoon freshly grated nutmeg
- 2 sticks unsalted butter, softened
- 1 cup granulated sugar
- ½ cup packed light brown sugar
- 2 large eggs
- 2 teaspoons pure vanilla extract
- 2 cups old-fashioned rolled oats
- 1 cup Amarena or brandied sour cherries in syrup, drained

  Turbinado sugar, for sprinkling

Megan Garrelts, pastry chef at Bluestem in Kansas City, Missouri, grew up eating pies filled with cherries from her family's backyard tree. In this recipe, she combines the fruit with another classic American dessert, oatmeal cookies. Along with her husband (Bluestem's chef), Colby, she makes buttery oversize cookies with Amarena cherries or, for a more sophisticated recipe, brandied cherries.

1. Preheat the oven to 350° and position racks in the upper and lower thirds. Line 2 large baking sheets with parchment paper. In a medium bowl, whisk the flours with the baking soda, salt, cinnamon and nutmeg. In a large bowl, using an electric mixer, beat the butter with the granulated and brown sugars at medium-high speed until light and fluffy, about 5 minutes. Add the eggs and vanilla and beat until smooth. Add the dry ingredients and beat at low speed until combined. Add the oats and cherries and beat until the cherries are slightly mashed and evenly distributed.

2. Working in batches, scoop 6 scant ¼-cup balls of dough onto each of the prepared baking sheets, spacing them evenly, and sprinkle with turbinado sugar. Bake for 16 minutes, shifting the sheets from top to bottom and front to back halfway through, until dark golden brown. Let the cookies cool on the baking sheets for 5 minutes, then transfer to a rack to cool completely. Bake the remaining 6 cookies.

MAKE AHEAD The cookies can be kept in an airtight container at room temperature for up to 3 days or frozen for up to 1 month.

double and
FREEZE

rosemary-cornmeal sugar cookies

Active **45 min**; Total **1 hr 30 min plus cooling**; Makes **about 6 dozen cookies**

- 1½ **cups all-purpose flour**
- 1½ **cups fine yellow cornmeal**
- ¼ **cup nonfat dry milk powder**
- ¾ **teaspoon baking powder**
- ¼ **teaspoon baking soda**
- 4 **teaspoons finely chopped rosemary**
- 1 **teaspoon salt**
- ¾ **cup fresh or thawed frozen corn kernels**
- 2 **teaspoons finely grated lemon zest**
- 2½ **sticks unsalted butter, at room temperature**
- ¾ **cup plus 3 tablespoons sugar**
- 1 **large egg**
- ¼ **cup sorghum molasses or dark honey**
- 2 **teaspoons fresh lemon juice**
- 1 **teaspoon pure vanilla extract**

Chef **Tim Byres** of Smoke in Dallas mixes fresh rosemary into cornmeal cookies, giving them a fabulous savory note. The recipe can be made two ways: as drop cookies or the slice-and-bake kind for a crisper texture.

1. Preheat the oven to 350°. Line 2 large baking sheets with parchment paper. In a medium bowl, whisk the flour, cornmeal, milk powder, baking powder, baking soda, rosemary and ½ teaspoon of the salt.

2. In a food processor, pulse the corn with the lemon zest until very finely chopped.

3. In the bowl of a standing mixer fitted with the paddle, beat the butter with ¾ cup of the sugar at medium-high speed for 2 minutes, until smooth. Beat in the egg until incorporated. At low speed, beat in the chopped corn mixture, then add the molasses, lemon juice and vanilla. Beat at high speed until pale and fluffy, about 5 minutes. At low speed, beat in the dry ingredients in 3 additions.

4. Working in 2 batches, scoop 1¼-inch mounds of dough onto the prepared baking sheets, about 2 inches apart. With damp fingers, flatten each mound slightly. In a small bowl, mix the remaining 3 tablespoons of sugar and ½ teaspoon of salt and sprinkle half of the mixture on the cookies. Bake in the upper and lower thirds of the oven for 12 to 15 minutes, until golden brown; shift the pans from top to bottom and front to back halfway through. Slide the parchment paper from the baking sheets onto racks. Repeat to bake the remaining dough.

VARIATION For a slice-and-bake version of these cookies, refrigerate the dough for 30 minutes, until no longer sticky. Form it into 2 logs, 2½ inches in diameter. Wrap tightly in plastic and freeze until firm or for up to 1 month. Slice the logs ¼ inch thick and proceed as above.

dark chocolate pudding

Total **35 min plus chilling**

Serves **4**

⅔ cup sugar

1½ teaspoons cornstarch

1½ teaspoons unsweetened cocoa powder

½ teaspoon salt

4 ounces bittersweet chocolate, finely chopped (1 cup)

1 tablespoon unsalted butter

1½ cups whole milk

½ cup heavy cream

3 large egg yolks

Whipped cream, for serving

Chef Spike Gjerde makes this rich version of the childhood favorite at Shoo-Fly Diner in Baltimore. Since the pudding has so few ingredients, he insists that they be of high quality: For the chocolate, Gjerde likes Mast Brothers Brooklyn Blend but says to use your favorite dark chocolate (about 70 percent or higher). For the cocoa powder, he prefers Valrhona.

1. In a medium bowl, whisk the sugar with the cornstarch, cocoa and salt. In a large bowl, combine the chocolate and butter.

2. In a medium saucepan, heat the milk and cream over moderate heat just until bubbles form around the edge of the pan; remove from the heat. Whisk ½ cup of the hot milk into the sugar mixture, then whisk in the egg yolks and another ½ cup of the hot milk. Return the mixture to the saucepan and cook over moderate heat, whisking constantly, until bubbles begin to form around the edge of the pan and a candy thermometer inserted in the pudding registers 165°, about 5 minutes.

3. Strain the pudding into the bowl with the chocolate and butter and whisk until incorporated, about 2 minutes. Press a sheet of plastic wrap directly onto the surface of the pudding and refrigerate until chilled, about 2 hours. Scoop into bowls and serve with whipped cream.

MAKE AHEAD The pudding can be refrigerated for up to 2 days.

> For one family movie night, my son asked for the popcorn pot de crème from my restaurant. We started messing around in the kitchen, and popcorn pudding is now a part of all our movie nights.

JONATHON SAWYER

popcorn pudding

Total **30 min plus chilling**

Serves **6**

2¼ cups whole milk

¾ cup heavy cream

½ cup sugar

¼ teaspoon salt

1 teaspoon vegetable oil

¼ cup plus 1 tablespoon popcorn kernels

3 large egg yolks

4 teaspoons cornstarch

3 tablespoons unsalted butter, cubed

¼ teaspoon pure vanilla extract

Jonathon Sawyer and his family love the sweet-salty contrast of chocolate-covered pretzels. That gave Sawyer, chef at Cleveland's Greenhouse Tavern, the idea to create this velvety dessert: He brilliantly combines the flavor of buttered popcorn with a sweet, creamy vanilla pudding.

1. In a large saucepan, combine the milk, cream, sugar and salt and bring to a boil over moderate heat, stirring to dissolve the sugar. Remove from the heat.

2. In a medium pot, heat the oil. Add the popcorn kernels, cover and cook over moderate heat until they start popping. Cook, shaking the pot constantly, until the popping has almost stopped, 2 to 3 minutes. Pour all but 1 cup of the popcorn into the cream mixture, cover and let stand for 10 minutes. Reserve the remaining popcorn for garnish.

3. In a medium bowl, whisk the egg yolks with the cornstarch until smooth. Strain the hot cream mixture into a clean medium saucepan; discard the solids. Bring the cream to a boil over moderate heat. Gradually whisk 1 cup of the hot cream into the egg yolks, then scrape the mixture into the saucepan. Whisk the pudding over moderate heat until it just comes to a boil, about 2 minutes. Stir in the butter and vanilla.

4. Scrape the pudding into a medium baking dish. Press a piece of plastic wrap directly onto the surface of the pudding and refrigerate until chilled. Spoon the pudding into bowls, sprinkle with the reserved cup of popcorn and serve.

FARRO & Chickpea soup
Pozole
POPCORN PUDDING
BRAISED CHICKEN
DAL
SEAFOOD STEW
CHICKEN HOT POT

index

A

ANCHOVIES
Crisp Pan-Roasted Chicken with
    Anchovies, Capers and Lemon, 22
Kale Caesar Salad, 154
Red Snapper with Asparagus and
    Chorizo, 123
Rigatoni with Clams, Sausage and
    Broccoli Rabe, 196
Roast Salmon with Lemony Basil
    Sauce, 127

APPLES
Fruit and Nut Crumb Bars, 218
Red Kuri Squash Soup with Ancho
    Chile and Apple, 172

APRICOTS
Sautéed Pork Tenderloin with Apricots
    and Mustard, 67

ARUGULA
Sea Bass Piccata with Fried Capers
    and Leeks, 116
Trout Amandine with
    Creamy Spinach, 115

ASPARAGUS
Creamy Pasta with Chicken and
    Vegetables, 192
Red Snapper with Asparagus and
    Chorizo, 123
Sweet and Savory Summer Fruit Salad
    with Blue Cheese, 159

AVOCADOS
Flash-Fried Chicken Carnitas, 32
Goat Cheese and Avocado Toasts, 210
Sweet and Savory Summer Fruit Salad
    with Blue Cheese, 159
Chipotle-Braised Chicken Thighs
    with Poached Eggs, 37

B

BACON
Bacon and Egg Fried Rice, 204
Creamy Shrimp, Corn and
    Tomato Chowder, 138
Cuban Frittata with Bacon and
    Potatoes, 214

BASIL
Creamy Pasta with Chicken and
    Vegetables, 192
Grilled Chicken with Miso-Basil
    Marinade, 29
Pizza with Baked Meatballs, 209
Roast Salmon with Lemony
    Basil Sauce, 127
Sweet Potato Cakes with Yellow Corn,
    Basil and Goat Cheese, 166
Winter Vegetable Minestrone, 177

BEANS. See also CHICKPEAS;
GREEN BEANS; LENTILS
Chipotle-Braised Chicken Thighs
    with Poached Eggs, 37
Healthy Chicken Jambalaya, 49
Kale, Black Bean and Red Chile Tacos
    with Queso Fresco, 168
Quinoa Salad with Spring
    Vegetables, 156
"Steak Bomb" Rice and Beans, 90
Thai Chicken Soup, 50
Winter Vegetable Minestrone, 177

BEEF
Beef, Turkey and Mushroom
    Meat Loaf, 92
California Steak Salad, 82
Flank Steak with Chimichurri, 86
Grilled Strip Steaks with Green Bean
    Chimichurri, 80

Mapo Tofu, 74
Peruvian-Style Pasta Bolognese, 186
Pizza with Baked Meatballs, 209
Rib Eye Steaks with Grilled
    Radicchio, 89
Skirt Steak with Roasted
    Tomatillo Salsa, 85
"Steak Bomb" Rice and Beans, 90

BERRIES
Roast Chicken Panzanella, 53
Sweet and Savory Summer Fruit Salad
    with Blue Cheese, 159

BREAD
Goat Cheese and Avocado Toasts, 210
Kale Caesar Salad, 154
Roast Chicken Panzanella, 53

BROCCOLI
Bacon and Egg Fried Rice, 204
Kitchen-Sink Soba Noodles, 160
Broccoli Rabe, Rigatoni with Clams,
    Sausage and, 196
Burgers, Provençal Lamb, 105

C

CABBAGE
Green Curry Shrimp Lettuce Bowl, 135

CAKES
Brown Sugar Crumb Cake, 224
Mexican Chocolate Chip–Pumpkin
    Seed Cake, 226
Rhubarb Pudding Cake, 223

CAPERS
Cauliflower Steaks with
    Herb Salsa Verde, 163
Crisp Branzino with Spinach, 118
Crisp Pan-Roasted Chicken with
    Anchovies, Capers and Lemon, 22
Flank Steak with Chimichurri, 86
Roast Salmon with Lemony Basil
    Sauce, 127
Sea Bass Piccata with Fried Capers
    and Leeks, 116

CARROTS
Bacon and Egg Fried Rice, 204
Butcher Shop Chicken, 25
Farro and Chickpea Soup with
    Chicken Meatballs, 207
Italian Sausage Salad, 77

Kitchen-Sink Soba Noodles, 160
Lentils with Butternut Squash and
    Merguez Sausage, 106
Red Coconut Curry with Seafood and
    Mixed Vegetables, 146
Winter Vegetable Minestrone, 177

CAULIFLOWER
Cauliflower and Ricotta Mac
    and Cheese, 190
Cauliflower Steaks with Herb Salsa
    Verde, 163
Kitchen-Sink Soba Noodles, 160
Thai Chicken Soup, 50

CELERY
Butcher Shop Chicken, 25
Sausage Jambalaya, 203
Winter Vegetable Minestrone, 177

CHEESE. See also PARMESAN
Baked Polenta Casserole, 213
Baked Rigatoni with Eggplant,
    Tomatoes and Ricotta, 189
California Steak Salad, 82
Cauliflower and Ricotta Mac and
    Cheese, 190
Cheese Enchiladas with Red
    Chile Sauce, 171
Goat Cheese and Avocado Toasts, 210
Kale, Black Bean and Red Chile Tacos
    with Queso Fresco, 168
Orecchiette with Summer Squash,
    Mint and Goat Cheese, 199
Peruvian-Style Arroz con Pollo, 46
Provençal Lamb Burgers, 105
Rigatoni with Lemony Kale-and-
    Pecorino Pesto, 195
Shrimp and Wild Mushroom
    Risotto, 200
Spiced-Lamb and Potato Pie, 102
"Steak Bomb" Rice and Beans, 90
Sweet and Savory Summer Fruit Salad
    with Blue Cheese, 159
Sweet Potato Cakes with Yellow Corn,
    Basil and Goat Cheese, 166

CHERRIES
Oatmeal-Cherry Cookies, 229

CHICKEN
Beer-Braised Chicken Wings with
    Clams and Chickpeas, 43
Butcher Shop Chicken, 25

Chicken Hot Pot, 40
Chipotle-Braised Chicken Thighs with
    Poached Eggs, 37
Creamy Pasta with Chicken and
    Vegetables, 192
Crisp Pan-Roasted Chicken with
    Anchovies, Capers and Lemon, 22
Crispy Chicken Cutlets with Swiss
    Chard, 31
Crunchy Baked Chicken Thighs with
    Grainy Mustard and Garlic, 26
Farro and Chickpea Soup with
    Chicken Meatballs, 207
Flash-Fried Chicken Carnitas, 32
Grilled Chicken with Miso-Basil
    Marinade, 29
Healthy Chicken Jambalaya, 49
Herb-Roasted Spatchcock Chicken, 21
JW Fried Chicken, 34
Peruvian-Style Arroz con Pollo, 46
Roast Chicken Panzanella, 53
Tangy Chicken Adobo, 38
Thai Chicken Soup, 50
Turmeric Chicken and Rice, 44

CHICKPEAS
Beer-Braised Chicken Wings with
    Clams and Chickpeas, 43
Chickpea-Vegetable Stew, 175
Farro and Chickpea Soup with
    Chicken Meatballs, 207
Spicy Shrimp with Pan-Seared
    Romaine and Chickpea Puree, 132

CHILES. See also PEPPERS
Chipotle-Braised Chicken Thighs with
    Poached Eggs, 37
Flash-Fried Chicken Carnitas, 32
Ginger-Braised Pork Meatballs in
    Coconut Broth, 68
Green Curry Shrimp Lettuce Bowl, 135
Healthy Chicken Jambalaya, 49
Jumbo Shrimp with Garlic and Chile
    Butter, 136
Kale, Black Bean and Red Chile Tacos
    with Queso Fresco, 168
Lamb Shoulder Steaks with
    Ratatouille, 101
Pork and Chorizo Pozole, 64
Red Kuri Squash Soup with Ancho
    Chile and Apple, 172

Seared Sole with Lime Sauce, 112
Skirt Steak with Roasted Tomatillo
    Salsa, 85
Thai Chicken Soup, 50
CHOCOLATE
Dark Chocolate Pudding, 232
Mexican Chocolate Chip–Pumpkin
    Seed Cake, 226
CILANTRO
Flash-Fried Chicken Carnitas, 32
Green Curry Shrimp Lettuce Bowl, 135
Grilled Strip Steaks with Green Bean
    Chimichurri, 80
Jumbo Shrimp with Garlic and Chile
    Butter, 136
Peruvian Seafood and Rice Stew, 149
Peruvian-Style Arroz con Pollo, 46
Red Coconut Curry with Seafood and
    Mixed Vegetables, 146
Roast Chicken Panzanella, 53
Seared Sole with Lime Sauce, 112
Skirt Steak with Roasted
    Tomatillo Salsa, 85
Thai Chicken Soup, 50
CLAMS
Beer-Braised Chicken Wings with
    Clams and Chickpeas, 43
Manila Clams with Lentils
    and Kale, 143
Rigatoni with Clams, Sausage and
    Broccoli Rabe, 196
Cobbler, Roasted Peach, with Vanilla
Ice Cream and Balsamic Syrup, 221
COCONUT MILK
Chickpea-Vegetable Stew, 175
Ginger-Braised Pork Meatballs in
    Coconut Broth, 68
Green Curry Shrimp Lettuce Bowl, 135
Red Coconut Curry with Seafood
    and Mixed Vegetables, 146
Thai Chicken Soup, 50
COOKIES AND BARS
Fruit and Nut Crumb Bars, 218
Oatmeal-Cherry Cookies, 229
Rosemary-Cornmeal Sugar
    Cookies, 230
CORN
Creamy Shrimp, Corn and Tomato
    Chowder, 138

Rosemary-Cornmeal Sugar
    Cookies, 230
Sweet and Savory Summer Fruit Salad
    with Blue Cheese, 159
Sweet Potato Cakes with Yellow Corn,
    Basil and Goat Cheese, 166
Crab Cakes, Maryland-Style, 150
CUCUMBERS
Grilled Lamb Chops with Cucumber
    Relish, 98
Italian Sausage Salad, 77
Quinoa-Crusted Salmon with Spicy
    Orange-Miso Sauce, 128
Roast Chicken Panzanella, 53

E

EGGPLANT
Baked Rigatoni with Eggplant,
    Tomatoes and Ricotta, 189
Lamb Shoulder Steaks with
    Ratatouille, 101
EGGS
Bacon and Egg Fried Rice, 204
Cheater's Ramen with Country Ham,
    Parmesan and Egg, 70
Chipotle-Braised Chicken Thighs
    with Poached Eggs, 37
Cuban Frittata with Bacon and
    Potatoes, 214
Roasted Root Vegetables with
    Fried Eggs, 165
Enchiladas, Cheese, with Red
Chile Sauce, 171

F

Farro and Chickpea Soup with
Chicken Meatballs, 207
FENNEL
Kitchen-Sink Soba Noodles, 160
Seafood, Tomato and
    Fennel Stew, 140
FISH. *See also* **ANCHOVIES**
Crisp Branzino with Spinach, 118
Halibut with Roasted Potatoes and
    Romanesco Salad, 125
Pan-Fried Flounder with Lemon
    Butter Sauce, 110

Quinoa-Crusted Salmon with Spicy
    Orange-Miso Sauce, 128
Red Coconut Curry with Seafood and
    Mixed Vegetables, 146
Red Snapper with Asparagus and
    Chorizo, 123
Roast Salmon with Lemony Basil
    Sauce, 127
Sea Bass Piccata with Fried Capers
    and Leeks, 116
Seafood, Tomato and
    Fennel Stew, 140
Seared Sole with Lime Sauce, 112
Trout Amandine with Creamy
    Spinach, 115
Tuna Steaks with Plums, 120
FISH SAUCE
Chicken-Fried Pork Chops, 58
Green Curry Shrimp Lettuce Bowl, 135
Halibut with Roasted Potatoes and
    Romanesco Salad, 125
Seared Sole with Lime Sauce, 112
Thai Chicken Soup, 50
Turmeric Chicken and Rice, 44
Frittata, Cuban, with Bacon and
Potatoes, 214

G

GARLIC
Baked Rigatoni with Eggplant,
    Tomatoes and Ricotta, 189
Crisp Branzino with Spinach, 118
Crunchy Baked Chicken Thighs with
    Grainy Mustard and Garlic, 26
Flank Steak with Chimichurri, 86
Grilled Chicken with Miso-Basil
    Marinade, 29
Herb-Roasted Spatchcock Chicken, 21
Jumbo Shrimp with Garlic and Chile
    Butter, 136
Peruvian-Style Pasta Bolognese, 186
Red Snapper with Asparagus and
    Chorizo, 123
Rigatoni with Clams, Sausage and
    Broccoli Rabe, 196
Seared Sole with Lime Sauce, 112
Spaghetti with Veal Meatballs, 182
Tangy Chicken Adobo, 38

GINGER

Bacon and Egg Fried Rice, 204

Cheater's Ramen with Country Ham, Parmesan and Egg, 70

Chicken Hot Pot, 40

Chickpea-Vegetable Stew, 175

Ginger-Braised Pork Meatballs in Coconut Broth, 68

Grilled Chicken with Miso-Basil Marinade, 29

Grilled Pork Chops with Ginger Sauce, 56

Kitchen-Sink Soba Noodles, 160

Peruvian-Style Pasta Bolognese, 186

Red Lentil Dal with Rice, Yogurt and Tomatoes, 178

Soy and Ginger Pork Chops, 61

Thai Chicken Soup, 50

GRAPES

Kale Caesar Salad, 154

GREEN BEANS

California Steak Salad, 82

Grilled Strip Steaks with Green Bean Chimichurri, 80

Red Coconut Curry with Seafood and Mixed Vegetables, 146

GREENS. See also specific greens

California Steak Salad, 82

Chicken Hot Pot, 40

Cuban Frittata with Bacon and Potatoes, 214

Farro and Chickpea Soup with Chicken Meatballs, 207

H

HAM. See also PANCETTA

Cheater's Ramen with Country Ham, Parmesan and Egg, 70

HERBS. See also specific herbs

Butcher Shop Chicken, 25

Cauliflower Steaks with Herb Salsa Verde, 163

Creamy Shrimp, Corn and Tomato Chowder, 138

Herb-Roasted Spatchcock Chicken, 21

Kale Caesar Salad, 154

Provençal Lamb Burgers, 105

Quinoa Salad with Spring Vegetables, 156

Roast Chicken Panzanella, 53

Roasted Root Vegetables with Fried Eggs, 165

Rosemary-Cornmeal Sugar Cookies, 230

Salt-Crusted Rack of Lamb, 96

Sautéed Pork Tenderloin with Apricots and Mustard, 67

K

KALE

Kale, Black Bean and Red Chile Tacos with Queso Fresco, 168

Kale Caesar Salad, 154

Manila Clams with Lentils and Kale, 143

Rigatoni with Lemony Kale-and-Pecorino Pesto, 195

L

LAMB

Grilled Lamb Chops with Cucumber Relish, 98

Lamb Shoulder Steaks with Ratatouille, 101

Lentils with Butternut Squash and Merguez Sausage, 106

Provençal Lamb Burgers, 105

Salt-Crusted Rack of Lamb, 96

Spiced-Lamb and Potato Pie, 102

LEEKS

Sea Bass Piccata with Fried Capers and Leeks, 116

Winter Vegetable Minestrone, 177

LEMONGRASS

Ginger-Braised Pork Meatballs in Coconut Broth, 68

Green Curry Shrimp Lettuce Bowl, 135

Thai Chicken Soup, 50

LEMONS AND LEMON JUICE

Cauliflower Steaks with Herb Salsa Verde, 163

Crisp Pan-Roasted Chicken with Anchovies, Capers and Lemon, 22

Kale Caesar Salad, 154

Lentils with Butternut Squash and Merguez Sausage, 106

Manila Clams with Lentils and Kale, 143

Pan-Fried Flounder with Lemon Butter Sauce, 110

Quinoa Salad with Spring Vegetables, 156

Red Snapper with Asparagus and Chorizo, 123

Rigatoni with Lemony Kale-and-Pecorino Pesto, 195

Roast Salmon with Lemony Basil Sauce, 127

LENTILS

Chorizo with Rice and Lentils, 73

Lentils with Butternut Squash and Merguez Sausage, 106

Manila Clams with Lentils and Kale, 143

Red Lentil Dal with Rice, Yogurt and Tomatoes, 178

LETTUCE

California Steak Salad, 82

Flash-Fried Chicken Carnitas, 32

Green Curry Shrimp Lettuce Bowl, 135

Italian Sausage Salad, 77

Roast Chicken Panzanella, 53

Spicy Shrimp with Pan-Seared Romaine and Chickpea Puree, 132

LIMES AND LIME JUICE

Flash-Fried Chicken Carnitas, 32

Green Curry Shrimp Lettuce Bowl, 135

Grilled Chicken with Miso-Basil Marinade, 29

Peruvian Seafood and Rice Stew, 149

Seared Sole with Lime Sauce, 112

Thai Chicken Soup, 50

M

Meat Loaf, Beef, Turkey and Mushroom, 92

MINT

Grilled Lamb Chops with Cucumber Relish, 98

Orecchiette with Summer Squash, Mint and Goat Cheese, 199

Spiced-Lamb and Potato Pie, 102

Sweet and Savory Summer Fruit Salad with Blue Cheese, 159

MISO
Cheater's Ramen with Country Ham, Parmesan and Egg, 70
Grilled Chicken with Miso-Basil Marinade, 29
Quinoa-Crusted Salmon with Spicy Orange-Miso Sauce, 128

MUSHROOMS
Beef, Turkey and Mushroom Meat Loaf, 92
Shrimp and Wild Mushroom Risotto, 200
"Steak Bomb" Rice and Beans, 90
Thai Chicken Soup, 50

MUSSELS
Mussels in a Saffron-Citrus Cream Sauce, 144
Peruvian Seafood and Rice Stew, 149
Red Coconut Curry with Seafood and Mixed Vegetables, 146
Seafood, Tomato and Fennel Stew, 140

MUSTARD
California Steak Salad, 82
Crunchy Baked Chicken Thighs with Grainy Mustard and Garlic, 26
Sautéed Pork Tenderloin with Apricots and Mustard, 67
Tuna Steaks with Plums, 120

N

NOODLES
Cheater's Ramen with Country Ham, Parmesan and Egg, 70
Chicken Hot Pot, 40
Kitchen-Sink Soba Noodles, 160

NUTS
Brown Sugar Crumb Cake, 224
Fruit and Nut Crumb Bars, 218
Green Curry Shrimp Lettuce Bowl, 135
Grilled Lamb Chops with Cucumber Relish, 98
Rigatoni with Lemony Kale-and-Pecorino Pesto, 195
Trout Amandine with Creamy Spinach, 115

O

OATS
Brown Sugar Crumb Cake, 224
Fruit and Nut Crumb Bars, 218
Oatmeal-Cherry Cookies, 229

OLIVES
Halibut with Roasted Potatoes and Romanesco Salad, 125
Provençal Lamb Burgers, 105

ONIONS
Bacon and Egg Fried Rice, 204
Chickpea-Vegetable Stew, 175
Cuban Frittata with Bacon and Potatoes, 214

ORANGES AND ORANGE JUICE
Kitchen-Sink Soba Noodles, 160
Quinoa-Crusted Salmon with Spicy Orange-Miso Sauce, 128
Seafood, Tomato and Fennel Stew, 140

P

PANCETTA
Bucatini all'Amatriciana with Parmigiano, 185

PARMESAN
Baked Rigatoni with Eggplant, Tomatoes and Ricotta, 189
Cheater's Ramen with Country Ham, Parmesan and Egg, 70
Creamy Pasta with Chicken and Vegetables, 192
Kale Caesar Salad, 154
Lamb Shoulder Steaks with Ratatouille, 101
Peruvian-Style Pasta Bolognese, 186
Pizza with Baked Meatballs, 209
Spaghetti with Veal Meatballs, 182
Tuna Steaks with Plums, 120
Winter Vegetable Minestrone, 177

PARSLEY
Cauliflower Steaks with Herb Salsa Verde, 163
Crisp Pan-Roasted Chicken with Anchovies, Capers and Lemon, 22
Flank Steak with Chimichurri, 86

Grilled Strip Steaks with Green Bean Chimichurri, 80
Halibut with Roasted Potatoes and Romanesco Salad, 125
Pizza with Baked Meatballs, 209
Roast Salmon with Lemony Basil Sauce, 127
Seafood, Tomato and Fennel Stew, 140

PASTA. *See also* **NOODLES**
Baked Rigatoni with Eggplant, Tomatoes and Ricotta, 189
Bucatini all'Amatriciana with Parmigiano, 185
Cauliflower and Ricotta Mac and Cheese, 190
Creamy Pasta with Chicken and Vegetables, 192
Orecchiette with Summer Squash, Mint and Goat Cheese, 199
Peruvian-Style Pasta Bolognese, 186
Rigatoni with Clams, Sausage and Broccoli Rabe, 196
Rigatoni with Lemony Kale-and-Pecorino Pesto, 195
Spaghetti with Veal Meatballs, 182

PEACHES
Roasted Peach Cobbler with Vanilla Ice Cream and Balsamic Syrup, 221
Sweet and Savory Summer Fruit Salad with Blue Cheese, 159

PEAS
Bacon and Egg Fried Rice, 204
California Steak Salad, 82
Peruvian-Style Arroz con Pollo, 46
Quinoa Salad with Spring Vegetables, 156
Red Coconut Curry with Seafood and Mixed Vegetables, 146
Spiced-Lamb and Potato Pie, 102

PEPPERS. *See also* **CHILES**
Bacon and Egg Fried Rice, 204
Chickpea-Vegetable Stew, 175
Green Curry Shrimp Lettuce Bowl, 135
Healthy Chicken Jambalaya, 49
Lamb Shoulder Steaks with Ratatouille, 101
Sausage Jambalaya, 203
"Steak Bomb" Rice and Beans, 90

PESTO
Baked Rigatoni with Eggplant,
    Tomatoes and Ricotta, 189
Rigatoni with Lemony Kale-and-
    Pecorino Pesto, 195

PICKLES
Cauliflower Steaks with Herb
    Salsa Verde, 163
Pie, Spiced-Lamb and Potato, 102
Pizza with Baked Meatballs, 209
Plums, Tuna Steaks with, 120
Polenta Casserole, Baked, 213
Popcorn Pudding, 235

PORK
Chicken-Fried Pork Chops, 58
Ginger-Braised Pork Meatballs
    in Coconut Broth, 68
Grilled Pork Chops with
    Ginger Sauce, 56
Mapo Tofu, 74
Pork and Chorizo Pozole, 64
Pork Blade Steaks with Sage Butter
    Sauce, 62
Sautéed Pork Tenderloin with Apricots
    and Mustard, 67
Soy and Ginger Pork Chops, 61

POTATOES
Chickpea-Vegetable Stew, 175
Creamy Shrimp, Corn and Tomato
    Chowder, 138
Cuban Frittata with Bacon and
    Potatoes, 214
Halibut with Roasted Potatoes and
    Romanesco Salad, 125
Seafood, Tomato and
    Fennel Stew, 140
Spiced-Lamb and Potato Pie, 102

PUDDINGS
Dark Chocolate Pudding, 232
Popcorn Pudding, 235

PUMPKIN SEEDS
Mexican Chocolate Chip–Pumpkin
    Seed Cake, 226
Red Kuri Squash Soup with Ancho
    Chile and Apple, 172
Roast Chicken Panzanella, 53

Q

QUINOA
Quinoa-Crusted Salmon with Spicy
    Orange-Miso Sauce, 128
Quinoa Salad with Spring
    Vegetables, 156

R

Radicchio, Grilled, Rib Eye
    Steaks with, 89

RADISHES
California Steak Salad, 82
Quinoa Salad with Spring
    Vegetables, 156
Sweet and Savory Summer Fruit Salad
    with Blue Cheese, 159
Rhubarb Pudding Cake, 223

RICE
Bacon and Egg Fried Rice, 204
Chorizo with Rice and Lentils, 73
Healthy Chicken Jambalaya, 49
Peruvian Seafood and Rice Stew, 149
Peruvian-Style Arroz con Pollo, 46
Red Lentil Dal with Rice, Yogurt and
    Tomatoes, 178
Sausage Jambalaya, 203
Shrimp and Wild Mushroom
    Risotto, 200
"Steak Bomb" Rice and Beans, 90
Turmeric Chicken and Rice, 44
Romanesco Salad, Halibut with Roasted
    Potatoes and, 125

S

Saffron-Citrus Cream Sauce,
    Mussels in, 144

SAGE
Farro and Chickpea Soup with
    Chicken Meatballs, 207
Pork Blade Steaks with Sage
    Butter Sauce, 62

SALADS
California Steak Salad, 82
Italian Sausage Salad, 77
Kale Caesar Salad, 154

Quinoa Salad with Spring
    Vegetables, 156
Roast Chicken Panzanella, 53
Sweet and Savory Summer Fruit Salad
    with Blue Cheese, 159

SALSA
Cauliflower Steaks with Herb
    Salsa Verde, 163
Peruvian Seafood and Rice Stew, 149
Skirt Steak with Roasted Tomatillo
    Salsa, 85

SAUSAGES
Chorizo with Rice and Lentils, 73
Healthy Chicken Jambalaya, 49
Italian Sausage Salad, 77
Pork and Chorizo Pozole, 64
Red Snapper with Asparagus and
    Chorizo, 123
Rigatoni with Clams, Sausage and
    Broccoli Rabe, 196
Sausage Jambalaya, 203

SCALLIONS
Cheese Enchiladas with Red
    Chile Sauce, 171
Chorizo with Rice and Lentils, 73
Kitchen-Sink Soba Noodles, 160
Sausage Jambalaya, 203

SCALLOPS
Peruvian Seafood and Rice Stew, 149

SESAME SEEDS
Crispy Chicken Cutlets with Swiss
    Chard, 31
Kitchen-Sink Soba Noodles, 160
Spicy Shrimp with Pan-Seared
    Romaine and Chickpea Puree, 132

SHELLFISH. *See specific shellfish*
SHRIMP
Creamy Shrimp, Corn and Tomato
    Chowder, 138
Green Curry Shrimp Lettuce Bowl, 135
Jumbo Shrimp with Garlic and Chile
    Butter, 136
Peruvian Seafood and Rice Stew, 149
Red Coconut Curry with Seafood and
    Mixed Vegetables, 146
Seafood, Tomato and
    Fennel Stew, 140
Shrimp and Wild Mushroom
    Risotto, 200

Spicy Shrimp with Pan-Seared
    Romaine and Chickpea Puree, 132
SOUPS
Cheater's Ramen with Country Ham,
    Parmesan and Egg, 70
Chicken Hot Pot, 40
Creamy Shrimp, Corn and Tomato
    Chowder, 138
Farro and Chickpea Soup with
    Chicken Meatballs, 207
Red Kuri Squash Soup with Ancho
    Chile and Apple, 172
Thai Chicken Soup, 50
Winter Vegetable Minestrone, 177
SPINACH
Creamy Pasta with Chicken and
    Vegetables, 192
Crisp Branzino with Spinach, 118
Trout Amandine with Creamy
    Spinach, 115
SQUASH. See also ZUCCHINI
Lentils with Butternut Squash and
    Merguez Sausage, 106
Orecchiette with Summer Squash,
    Mint and Goat Cheese, 199
Red Kuri Squash Soup with Ancho
    Chile and Apple, 172
Roasted Root Vegetables with
    Fried Eggs, 165
SQUID
Peruvian Seafood and Rice Stew, 149
STEWS
Chickpea-Vegetable Stew, 175
Peruvian Seafood and Rice Stew, 149
Seafood, Tomato and
    Fennel Stew, 140
Sweet Potato Cakes with Yellow Corn,
    Basil and Goat Cheese, 166
SWISS CHARD
Crispy Chicken Cutlets with Swiss
    Chard, 31
Kitchen-Sink Soba Noodles, 160

T

TOFU
Kitchen-Sink Soba Noodles, 160
Mapo Tofu, 74

TOMATILLOS
Pork and Chorizo Pozole, 64
Skirt Steak with Roasted Tomatillo
    Salsa, 85
TOMATOES
Baked Rigatoni with Eggplant,
    Tomatoes and Ricotta, 189
Bucatini all'Amatriciana with
    Parmigiano, 185
Butcher Shop Chicken, 25
Chipotle-Braised Chicken Thighs with
    Poached Eggs, 37
Creamy Shrimp, Corn and Tomato
    Chowder, 138
Flash-Fried Chicken Carnitas, 32
Goat Cheese and Avocado Toasts, 210
Jumbo Shrimp with Garlic and Chile
    Butter, 136
Lamb Shoulder Steaks with
    Ratatouille, 101
Lentils with Butternut Squash and
    Merguez Sausage, 106
Peruvian Seafood and Rice Stew, 149
Peruvian-Style Pasta Bolognese, 186
Pizza with Baked Meatballs, 209
Pork and Chorizo Pozole, 64
Red Lentil Dal with Rice, Yogurt and
    Tomatoes, 178
Roast Chicken Panzanella, 53
Sausage Jambalaya, 203
Sautéed Pork Tenderloin with Apricots
    and Mustard, 67
Seafood, Tomato and
    Fennel Stew, 140
Spaghetti with Veal Meatballs, 182
Winter Vegetable Minestrone, 177
Turkey, Beef and Mushroom
    Meat Loaf, 92
Turmeric Chicken and Rice, 44

V

Veal Meatballs, Spaghetti with, 182
**VEGETABLES. See also specific
vegetables**
Bacon and Egg Fried Rice, 204
Chicken Hot Pot, 40
Creamy Pasta with Chicken and
    Vegetables, 192

Peruvian-Style Arroz con Pollo, 46
Red Coconut Curry with Seafood
    and Mixed Vegetables, 146
Roasted Root Vegetables with
    Fried Eggs, 165
Winter Vegetable Minestrone, 177
VINEGAR
Pork Blade Steaks with Sage
    Butter Sauce, 62
Roasted Peach Cobbler with Vanilla
    Ice Cream and Balsamic Syrup, 221
Tangy Chicken Adobo, 38

W

WATERCRESS
California Steak Salad, 82
Cuban Frittata with Bacon and
    Potatoes, 214

Y

YOGURT
Crispy Chicken Cutlets with Swiss
    Chard, 31
Red Lentil Dal with Rice, Yogurt
    and Tomatoes, 178
Sweet and Savory Summer Fruit Salad
    with Blue Cheese, 159

Z

ZUCCHINI
Lamb Shoulder Steaks with
    Ratatouille, 101
Orecchiette with Summer Squash,
    Mint and Goat Cheese, 199

> If you're cooking at home while balancing a busy life, but you're giving it a good college try, be nice to yourself. I bet the food tastes better than you think. —Alex Guarnaschelli

style guide

credits

COVER AND FRONT OF BOOK
Apron from Too Strong USA,
toostrongusa.com. **P. 11** Flatware from
TableArt, *tableartonline.com.*

CHICKEN
P. 19 Decoupage tray from John Derian,
johnderian.com. **P. 20** Steel griddle from
Lodge, *lodgemfg.com.* **P. 23** Plate by Jars
from Didriks, *didriks.com.*
P. 30 Platter by Jan Burtz from ABC
Carpet & Home, *abchome.com.*
P. 36 Pot by Sambonet,
sambonet-shop.com; napkin from Auntie
Oti, *auntieoti.com.* **P. 39** Glasses from
Kate Spade Saturday, *saturday.com.*
P. 41 Bowl from Middle Kingdom,
middlekingdomporcelain.com.
P. 42 Bowls from Middle Kingdom,
middlekingdomporcelain.com; deep sauté
pan from West Elm, *westelm.com.*
P. 45 Plates by Potomak, *potomak.it;*
glasses by Norm Architects from Menu,
menudesignshop.com. **P. 47** Napkin by
Bella Notte Linens, *bellanottelinens.com.*
P. 51 Bowl by Humble Ceramics,
humbleceramics.com.

PORK
P. 54 Ladle by Cutipol from Mud
Australia, *us.mudaustralia.com.*
P. 57 Serving platter by Brickett Davda,

brickettdavda.com. **P. 59** Plate by Jars
from Didriks, *didriks.com.* **P. 63** Plates
from Mud Australia, *us.mudaustralia
.com.* **P. 65** Bowls by Humble Ceramics,
humbleceramics.com. **P. 66** Pasta plate
by Urban Oasis from ABC Carpet &
Home, *abchome.com.* **P. 69** Bowls by
Jars from Didriks, *didriks.com.*
P. 70 Bowls by Urban Oasis from
Lekker Home, *lekkerhome.com.*
P. 75 Braising skillet by Borough
Furnace, *boroughfurnace.com.*
P. 76 Wooden spice bowl by Josh Vogel
for March, *marchsf.com;* grill pan
from Lodge, *lodgemfg.com.*

BEEF
P. 79 Plates by Jan Burtz from
ABC Carpet & Home, *abchome.com.*
P. 83 Plate and bowl by Potomak,
potomak.it. **P. 87** Butcher block by
Geoffrey Lilge from OnOurTable,
onourtable.ca; knife by Stelton from
A + R, *aplusrstore.com.* **P. 93** Glasses
by Nouvel Studio, *nouvelstudio.com;* salt
dish by Hasami Porcelain from Tortoise
General Store, *tortoisegeneralstore.com.*

LAMB
P. 97 Board by Lostine from Minam,
minam.com. **P. 99** Plate by Humble
Ceramics, *humbleceramics.com.*

P. 100 Braiser by Le Creuset,
lecreuset.com.
P. 103 Sauté pan from West Elm,
westelm.com. **P. 107** Saucepan by
Sambonet, *sambonet-shop.com.*

FISH
P. 113 Bowl by Fürstenberg from Fitzsu,
fitzsu.com. **P. 114** Platter from Mud
Australia, *us.mudaustralia.com.*
P. 117 Plates from Simon Pearce,
simonpearce.com. **P. 119** Plates from
Canvas Home, *canvashomestore.com;*
salt/pepper dishes by Humble
Ceramics, *humbleceramics.com.*
P. 121 Pan from West Elm, *westelm.com.*
P. 129 Plate by Urban Oasis from
Lekker Home, *lekkerhome.com.*

SHELLFISH
P. 139 Bowls from Canvas Home,
canvashomestore.com. **P. 141** Plate by
Brickett Davda, *brickettdavda.com.*
P. 142 Bowl from ABC Carpet & Home,
abchome.com. **P. 145** Braiser by Le
Creuset, *lecreuset.com.*
P. 147 Bowls by Jim Franco Ceramics,
jimfrancoceramics.com. **P. 148** Braiser
by Le Creuset, *lecreuset.com.*

VEGETABLES
P. 161 Bowl by Würtz from Sigmar,
sigmarlondon.com. **P. 162** Platter by
Jan Burtz from ABC Carpet & Home,
abchome.com. **P. 164** Pasta bowl by
dbO Home from ABC Carpet & Home,
abchome.com; fork from TableArt,
tableartonline.com. **P. 167** Plate by
Hasami Porcelain from Tortoise
General Store, *tortoisegeneralstore.com.*
P. 173 Bowls by dbO Home,
dbohome.com. **P. 174** Bowl by Jim Franco
Ceramics, *jimfrancoceramics.com.*
P. 176 Napkin by Restoration Hardware,
restorationhardware.com. **P. 179** Bowls
holding lentils and rice, plates holding
cilantro and pappadums by Elephant
Ceramics, *elephantceramics.com.*

PASTA AND MORE
P. 183 Kitchen towel by Libeco,
libecohomestores.com. **P. 184** Bowls by
Würtz from Sigmar, *sigmarlondon.com.*

P. 187 Bowls by Humble Ceramics, *humbleceramics.com*. P. 188 Cast-iron pans by Nobuho Miya from Tortoise General Store, *tortoisegeneralstore.com*; forks from TableArt, *tableartonline.com*. P. 191 Roasting dish by Revol from Didriks, *didriks.com*. P. 197 Vintage vase and lidded jar from The End of History, *theendofhistoryshop.blogspot.com*. P. 198 Kobenstyle server by Dansk from Lenox, *lenox.com*. P. 201 French oven by Le Creuset, *lecreuset.com*. P. 206 Dutch oven from West Elm, *westelm.com*; ladle by Cutipol from ABC Carpet & Home, *abchome.com*. P. 212 Roasting dish by Staub from Zwilling J.A. Henckels, *zwillingonline.com*; kitchen cloth from Fog Linen Work, *shop-foglinen.com*.

DESSERTS

P. 216 Bowl with spout by Gleena, *gleena.com*. P. 220 Baking dishes by Revol from Didriks, *didriks.com*. P. 222 Plates by Jan Burtz from ABC Carpet & Home, *abchome.com*. P. 225 Footed bowl by KleinReid, *kleinreid.com*; decoupage plate from John Derian, *johnderian.com*.

BACK OF BOOK

P. 236 Glass storage jars by Bormioli Rocco from Crate & Barrel, *crateandbarrel.com*. P. 244 Wallpaper by Manuel Canovas from Cowtan & Tout, *designs.cowtan.com*.

more books by F&W

To order, call 800-284-4145 or visit foodandwine.com/books

annual cookbook

More than 700 recipes from the world's best cooks, including culinary legends Paula Wolfert and Jacques Pépin and star chefs like Thomas Keller, Jamie Oliver and Nancy Silverton.

best of the best

Over 110 delicious recipes from the 25 best cookbooks of the year, chosen by FOOD & WINE after rigorous testing. Plus, more than 20 exclusive, never-before-published recipes.

cocktails

This special 10th anniversary edition features over 150 of the decade's best drink recipes and favorite party food from acclaimed mixologists and chefs. Plus an indispensable guide to cocktail basics and the top bars and lounges around the country.

wine guide

An essential, pocket-size guide focusing on the 500 best wineries in the United States, with over 1,000 stellar wines.

special thanks

Simon Andrews for his enthusiastic creative input; Barrett Washburne, Julian Hensarling and Darrell Taunt for their extraordinary efforts on the shoot

Columbia Products Studio

P. 225 Black-and-white photograph by Daniela Stallinger Photography